YOUR GUIDE TO
YOUR PERSONAL RECOVERY PLAN

THE
AUTISTIC
BURNOUT
WORKBOOK

DR. MEGAN ANNA NEFF

Neurodivergent Psychologist and
Creator of @Neurodivergent_Insights

ADAMS MEDIA

New York   Amsterdam/Antwerp   London   Toronto   Sydney   New Delhi

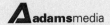

Adams Media
An Imprint of Simon & Schuster, LLC
100 Technology Center Drive
Stoughton, Massachusetts 02072

First Adams Media trade paperback edition March 2025

ADAMS MEDIA and colophon are registered trademarks
of Simon & Schuster, LLC.

For information about special discounts for bulk
purchases, please contact Simon & Schuster Special Sales
at 1-866-506-1949 or business@simonandschuster.com.

The Simon & Schuster Speakers Bureau can bring authors
to your live event. For more information or to book an event,
contact the Simon & Schuster Speakers Bureau at
1-866-248-3049 or visit our website at
www.simonspeakers.com.

Interior design by Priscilla Yuen
Interior images © 123RF; Adobe Stock

Manufactured in the United States of America

2 2025

ISBN 978-1-5072-2306-2

Contains material adapted from content available for purchase
through the author's website, NeurodivergentInsights.com.

CONTENTS

Introduction

BEING AUTISTIC is a huge part of who I am, and there's so much about it that I genuinely enjoy. I love the way my mind operates, the way I hold authenticity in such high regard, and the incredible way my thoughts build intricate webs of ideas and connections.

But I don't kid myself either—there are some aspects of being Autistic that can be pretty tough to handle. For me and many other Autistic people, one of the hardest parts is dealing with Autistic burnout and that constant feeling of low energy. I feel like I'm often at odds with my body, trying to find ways to get things done while my energy levels plummet.

Since recognizing my autism at the age of thirty-seven, I've embarked on a journey of exploration and innovation, striving to carve out a life beyond the shadows of burnout. This endeavor led to the creation of *Neurodivergent Insights*, a website where I've shared my experiences with and research about the nuances of wellness and resilience for Autistic and ADHD people. I wanted to adapt the psychological principles I'd been trained in as a clinical psychologist to work better for people like me (Autistic and/or ADHD people). How can we handle various sensory inputs, manage social situations, and rest and recharge effectively? I learned that the key to managing burnout was to make these concepts interactive—to reflect on my preferences, brainstorm ideas, make lists, map out my findings, and plan ahead for difficult moments.

The Autistic Burnout Workbook is a compilation of the best of the knowledge, visuals, and workbook pages that I created. It offers a comprehensive guide to navigating the complexities of burnout with a holistic lens.

> From navigating sleep practices and nervous system regulation to supporting sensory safety and setting healthy boundaries, I've realized that burnout often stems from vulnerabilities across multiple areas of our lives.

In each chapter, you'll find helpful background information about these key topics, along with various ways to personalize your healing, such as:

★ **Tracking your sensory likes and dislikes**

★ **Finding your energy igniters and zappers**

★ **Writing self-soothing statements to encourage sleep**

★ **Making a self-care plan for high-masking days**

The information, guidance, and interactive elements in this workbook will help you build a personal blueprint for Autistic burnout resilience. This proactive approach can help improve your mental health, promote self-care, and foster a sense of control in your day-to-day life. My hope is that this workbook helps you feel more empowered to build a life resilient to Autistic burnout!

How to Navigate This Book

MANY AUTISTIC individuals think in visuals. When I explore a topic deeply, my mind is drawn to—or creates its own!—images and diagrams that often explain the concept better than words can. Recognizing this, I've designed this book to be rich in visuals, to make the information more digestible, especially important during periods of burnout when our processing capabilities are diminished.

You can use this book in several different ways. Following the initial exploration of Autistic burnout in Chapter 1 and the recovery plan framework in Chapter 2, I encourage you to leap into whichever chapter speaks to you most directly, addressing the areas where you feel you could use the most support. Each chapter is designed to stand alone, so feel free to navigate the book in any order that resonates with you.

Some of the forms in this book are available as a free digital download at:

www.simonandschuster.com/p/autistic-burnout-workbook-excercises

Look for this image to find them.

That way, you can complete the form more than once and/or share it with loved ones.

AVAILABLE FOR DOWNLOAD

An important note: If you find yourself in the depths of severe burnout, to the point where reading and implementing even small changes seems daunting, it might be best to first seek support from a therapist or your medical team. Tackling burnout requires energy—a paradox that is particularly cruel!

To give you a clearer idea of what lies ahead, here's a brief overview of each chapter:

CHAPTER 1 lays the groundwork by exploring Autistic burnout in depth—its symptoms, its underlying causes, and what triggers it.

....

CHAPTER 2 introduces a comprehensive approach to recovering from Autistic burnout, presenting a holistic framework designed to support you on your journey. You will find guides that are meant to be filled out gradually as you build your recovery plan.

....

CHAPTER 3 dives into the realm of sensory regulation, providing tools to help you map out your sensory experiences.

....

CHAPTER 4 focuses on regulating the nervous system, offering guidance on how to track your nervous system's responses and techniques for soothing it.

CHAPTER 5 discusses various energy-management strategies, especially the spoon theory, aimed to help you manage your energy more sustainably.

....

CHAPTER 6 provides guidance on how to improve sleep quality and quantity, an integral element of burnout recovery.

....

CHAPTER 7 examines the intricate relationship between masking and burnout, alongside practical steps for gradual unmasking.

....

CHAPTER 8 emphasizes the critical role of self-advocacy and discusses how to effectively pursue accommodations, introducing the "self-advocacy equation." This chapter also covers the essential practice of setting and maintaining boundaries as a key aspect of burnout recovery.

Here are a few pointers for navigating this journey:

Assess your current energy levels at any given moment, and approach this process with that information in mind.

Pace yourself. It might be helpful to concentrate on a single chapter over a couple of months. Remember, burnout didn't appear overnight; similarly, building a life that feels balanced and fulfilling will take time.

Treat yourself with kindness and patience. You might find that you're able to implement some ideas easily and quickly, while others take practice or simply aren't for you; that's perfectly fine.

The bottom line is to use this workbook in any way that works for you—it's here to support and guide you on your personal recovery journey.

Acknowledgments

WHEN THE opportunity to write this book first came my way, I wasn't entirely sure if I should say yes. I mean, writing a book about burnout while balancing on my own tightrope between "okayness" and burnout felt like tempting fate. But I decided to go for it—though I couldn't have done it without the support of an incredible community that helped me honor my energy limits and maintain my balance.

First and foremost, thank you to my amazing spouse, Luke, who kept the home running so I could escape to sunny California for a few weeks in the dead of Oregon winter to write the first half of this book.

To my Neurodivergent Insights team: Betsy, thank you for stepping in to keep everything running smoothly and bringing order to my whirlwind of ideas. Jenny, your creative vision and fresh perspectives have brightened up so many of my projects. I'm deeply grateful to have you both on board.

To my editor, Laura, who helped organize my thoughts and streamline the vision I had for this project. Your guidance has been invaluable.

A heartfelt thank-you to the Autistic community at large, whose collective wisdom has enriched the conversation on Autistic burnout.

Special thanks to the members of the Learning Nook, who generously shared their metaphors and experiences. Your thoughtful, playful, and reflective conversations have enriched this book and made me a better thinker and human.

To Patrick Casale, my coconspirator on the *Divergent Conversations* podcast: Thank you for being a steadfast conversation partner. Your friendship has been a grounding force as I navigate the wonderfully messy world of public life in AuDHD space.

While I've never met them personally, I owe a deep debt of gratitude to Dr. Dora Raymaker and their research team for their pioneering work on Autistic burnout. Their research put the term on the clinical map, validating what the Autistic community has long discussed, and helped countless people (myself included) restructure their lives in ways that promote wellness rather than survival.

And finally, to anyone who's ever felt that particular combination of exhaustion, overstimulation, and "I just can't anymore"—this book is for you. Writing it taught me how to honor my limits, and reminded me that none of us are meant to do this alone.

CHAPTER 1

What Is Autistic Burnout?

Defining Autistic Burnout

The concept of Autistic burnout remains largely underexplored in traditional academic and clinical settings, which makes it difficult to define.

This oversight has resulted in a landscape where many professionals are unaware or ill prepared to address it effectively. Fortunately, the tide is turning, thanks in large part to the voices of Autistic self-advocates and the dedicated efforts of Autistic researchers who are further bringing to light the nuanced experiences of Autistic adults.

A landmark study in this evolving understanding is the groundbreaking work by Dr. Dora Raymaker and their team. Their 2020 study, "'Having All of Your Internal Resources Exhausted Beyond Measure and Being Left with No Clean-Up Crew': Defining Autistic Burnout," offers helpful insights into the reality of Autistic burnout. It not only defines the phenomenon with vivid clarity but also marks a critical step forward in acknowledging and addressing the challenges it presents. Raymaker and their colleagues were the first to put forward a clinical definition of Autistic burnout:

> Autistic burnout is a syndrome conceptualized as resulting from chronic life stress and **a mismatch of expectations and abilities without adequate supports**. It is characterized by pervasive, long-term (typically 3+ months) exhaustion, loss of function, and reduced tolerance to stimulus.
>
> —**DORA RAYMAKER ET AL.**, 2020 (emphasis added)

The following page features a visual summary of Raymaker et al.'s study. Do any of these findings resonate with your experience?

Key Findings from Raymaker's Research

 Autistic burnout arises from an accumulation of life's stressors becoming unbearable, particularly in the absence of accessible support.

 The relentless buildup of pressure creates a disparity where personal capabilities are eclipsed by external expectations.

 The repercussions of burnout are profound, affecting health, independence, and overall happiness. Alarmingly, it can escalate to self-harm or suicidal ideation and behavior.

 A common hurdle is the perceived lack of understanding and empathy from the non-Autistic community, which exacerbates the isolation felt by those experiencing burnout.

 Recovery is associated with self-acceptance, support networks, manageable expectations, and embracing one's Autistic identity.

Important Takeaways about Recovery

▶ Autistic burnout is distinct from job-related burnout or clinical depression, calling for tailored support strategies.

▶ Enhanced understanding of Autistic burnout paves the way for effective interventions, such as addressing Autistic masking and integrating burnout insights into suicide-prevention initiatives.

▶ Society must dismantle autism-related discrimination and stigma and foster a more inclusive and supportive environment.

SOURCE: Dora M. Raymaker et al., "'Having All of Your Internal Resources Exhausted Beyond Measure and Being Left with No Clean-Up Crew': Defining Autistic Burnout," *Autism in Adulthood* 2, no. 2 (June 2020): 132–143.

Core Features of Autistic Burnout

According to the Raymaker et al. study, Autistic burnout is characterized by three core elements that significantly impact daily functioning and well-being: chronic exhaustion, reduced tolerance to stimuli, and a loss of skills. Use the lines near each category to write down your experiences (or lack thereof) with that element.

CHRONIC EXHAUSTION

Burnout involves a pervasive sense of exhaustion that goes beyond basic physical weariness, extending into mental and emotional realms. This multifaceted fatigue infiltrates all aspects of daily life, rendering even basic tasks daunting. Crucially, this exhaustion isn't alleviated by a nap or a good night's sleep. It lingers stubbornly and affects overall quality of life.

_____

_____

REDUCED TOLERANCE TO STIMULI

During burnout, sensory sensitivities intensify. It's as if the world's volume has been amplified. Sounds, foods, textures, and transitions that were once manageable can become unmanageable during burnout.

_____

_____

LOSS OF SKILLS

Burnout can lead to a noticeable decline in a wide array of skills. This includes diminished executive functioning—the cognitive processes that govern planning, remembering, organizing, and executing tasks—as well as a decline in basic self-care and daily living activities. Verbal communication abilities may also suffer, adding to the complexity of the experience.

_____

_____

The Impact of Autistic Burnout on Your Life

Autistic burnout can wreak havoc on your life, leaving a profound impact in several ways. In a nutshell, Autistic burnout touches every facet of life, from health and daily functioning to personal relationships, parenting, and professional or academic achievements. Its lasting impact can span months or even years, significantly limiting participation in work, education, and social activities. Check any of these categories that apply to you.

PHYSICAL HEALTH: Burnout exacts a heavy toll on physical well-being, potentially contributing to chronic fatigue and a higher susceptibility to illnesses. Common physical manifestations include headaches, muscle tension, and a weakened immune system.

MENTAL HEALTH: Burnout can precipitate or exacerbate mental health conditions such as anxiety and depression. The relentless stress and fatigue overwhelm coping mechanisms, significantly impairing mental health.

DAILY LIVING: The capacity to manage day-to-day activities and live independently is often compromised. Routine tasks like personal hygiene, medication management, or meal preparation become overwhelmingly difficult. This decline in motivation and energy can lead to neglected self-care, further deteriorating physical and mental health.

RELATIONSHIPS: Burnout strains interpersonal connections with family, friends, children, and partners. The diminishment of energy and social capacity often leads to withdrawal and isolation, which can erode support networks and increase feelings of loneliness and frustration.

QUALITY OF LIFE: Burnout saps joy from daily activities and diminishes engagement with hobbies and interests. It creates a pervasive sense of living in a cycle of stress and exhaustion, where enthusiasm and motivation are absent.

WORK AND ACADEMICS: Professional and academic pursuits suffer as burnout drains cognitive resources and energy, resulting in decreased productivity and increased errors. The challenge of meeting deadlines and maintaining performance standards adds to the stress and anxiety and jeopardizes career or academic advancement.

SOURCE: Jane Mantzalas, Amanda L. Richdale, and Cheryl Dissanayake, "Examining Subjective Understandings of Autistic Burnout Using Q Methodology: A Study Protocol," *PLOS ONE* 18, no. 5 (May 2023).

Exploring Autistic Burnout Through Metaphor

Scientific definitions are valuable, but metaphors and people's lived experiences breathe life into understanding. Curious to further explore how burnout feels from the inside, I reached out to my community and gathered their insightful responses:

"Autistic burnout feels like barely keeping your own head above water while everyone else is having fun on Jet Skis above you."

"It's like running out of gas. In the middle of a busy road. And having to push your car home by yourself."

"Autistic burnout feels like playing the game of life on 'Hard Mode' while everyone else is playing the game on 'Easy Mode.'"

"I feel like I'm driving with my empty gas tank light on and have no idea if I'm going to make it to the next gas station in time."

E 〈⟶〉 F

"It feels like trying to run through the muck of a tidal flat while trying to stay ahead of the incoming tide and not being able to yell to someone for help."

Beyond metaphors, here are a few other ways that people described Autistic burnout:

"I have an extreme feeling of being untethered. Floating. Disoriented in all senses."

"Burnout feels like: I just . . . can't."

"Autistic burnout feels like all available energy goes into just barely surviving while everyone else is living life."

"For me, Autistic burnout feels like total and complete overwhelm and exhaustion. It's different than just being tired because I don't necessarily feel better after resting."

What Does Burnout Feel Like to You?

Now write down some examples of how *you* experience burnout—using metaphors, if possible. Reflect on each of the different categories you learned about—physical, mental, quality of life, professional/academic, daily living, and relationships.

The Differences Between Autistic Burnout and Other Forms of Burnout

You might have heard of burnout in non-Autistic situations. For example, occupational burnout is characterized by job-related exhaustion and depersonalization, whereas parental burnout involves intense fatigue and emotional detachment from parenting roles. Both are responses to specific stressors within their respective domains. However, **Autistic burnout encompasses a broader, more systemic exhaustion that is rooted in the cumulative stress of navigating a world that often feels alien**. To make things even more difficult, Autistic burnout can occur alongside and/or worsen occupational and parental burnout, if applicable, making the experience for Autistic individuals uniquely challenging. The essence of Autistic burnout lies in its pervasive impact, affecting an individual's ability to function across all areas of life.

A common challenge is the misunderstanding of Autistic burnout by friends and colleagues, who might not grasp its all-encompassing nature, often mistaking it for more familiar forms of burnout. **Misunderstood Autistic burnout leads to the minimization of Autistic experiences.** It's essential to communicate the comprehensive and profound effects of Autistic burnout.

Autistic burnout encompasses a broader, more systemic exhaustion that is rooted in the cumulative stress of *navigating a world that often feels alien*.

Autistic Burnout Can Mask Other Medical Conditions

It's essential to address the intersection between Autistic burnout and various medical conditions. For example, the similarities between Autistic burnout and conditions such as chronic fatigue syndrome, autoimmune disorders, and mast cell activation syndrome (MCAS) are both significant and complex.

Autistic physician Dr. Mel Houser describes this as "all the things" to encapsulate the experience many Autistic people face when they are diagnosed with a myriad of health issues. According to Houser, it's not uncommon for us to grapple with:

- Sleep disturbances
- Gastrointestinal troubles
- Connective tissue problems
- Immune system challenges
- Cardiovascular issues
- Post-viral illnesses

This broad spectrum of chronic conditions often mirrors the symptoms of Autistic burnout, making differentiating them challenging.

From personal experience, after my autism diagnosis, I initially attributed all my fatigue to burnout. It took time to recognize that underlying health issues, like long COVID and chronic fatigue syndrome, were being masked by what I perceived to simply be Autistic burnout. It's crucial to thoroughly investigate these symptoms, as conditions such as postural orthostatic tachycardia syndrome (POTS), long COVID, food sensitivities, and autoimmune disorders have specific treatments that can support your energy and wellness.

Be sure to work with your healthcare team to explore options if you are faced with chronic fatigue, gastrointestinal issues, or other pervasive symptoms beyond burnout. Paying close attention to potential factors like sleep disorders, autoimmune diseases, gastrointestinal disorders, and conditions like Ehlers-Danlos syndrome (EDS) or POTS is imperative.

The Complicated Connections Between Autistic Burnout and Depression

Depression and Autistic burnout are similar in many respects—but they also diverge in some critical ways. The Venn diagram on the next page illustrates both the overlap and the distinctions.

While it's important to recognize the similarities and differences, another key point is to understand that Autistic burnout often *leads* to depression and anxiety and even to suicidal thoughts or action. So, it's not an exaggeration to say that understanding and providing support for Autistic burnout can save lives.

Treatment Adaptations When Autistic Burnout and Depression Coexist

When Autistic burnout escalates and becomes a mood disorder such as depression or anxiety, it's vital that you work with a mental health professional, because you need a tailored approach to treatment when these conditions coexist. Treatment needs to also incorporate burnout recovery through rest. Here are some key therapy adaptations when burnout is present alongside depression:

 **BEHAVIORAL ACTIVATION:** *Behavioral activation is a common approach for treating depression that encourages structured activities to break the cycle of lethargy. However, when Autistic burnout and depression co-occur, it's critical to incorporate rest and honoring social limits into the treatment plan.*

 **COGNITIVE REFRAMING:** *This is a technique from cognitive behavioral therapy (CBT) that is aimed at reshaping negative thoughts. Yet, when applied to burnout, it requires a gentle touch to avoid exacerbating feelings of inadequacy or shame. It's important to navigate negative scripts with care, considering factors such as internalized ableism and the experience of grieving the limits of one's Autistic body (Autistic grief). Special attention should be given to ensure that CBT is not used in a way that invalidates the person's experience as a marginalized individual.*

Understanding Autistic Burnout and Depression:

A Venn Diagram

Autistic burnout can also look like depression; however, it needs to be supported differently. This Venn diagram highlights the overlap and differences. Also, an important thing to keep in mind is that a person can be experiencing both depression *and* Autistic burnout!

DEPRESSION

▶ **BEHAVIORAL ACTIVATION:** *Typically responds well to behavioral activation*

▶ **SLEEP CHANGES:** *May experience insomnia or excessive sleep*

▶ **ELEVATED SENSE OF WORTHLESSNESS:** *Intense sense of worthlessness*

▶ **DEPRESSED MOOD:** *Persistent depressed mood, lasting at least two weeks*

▶ **DEPRESSED MIND:** *Negative thoughts about the self, world, and future*

▶ **ANHEDONIA:** *Loss of pleasure in previously enjoyable activities*

▶ **SUICIDAL IDEATION:** *Thoughts and behaviors related to the desire to end one's life*

OVERLAP

▶ Concentration difficulties

▶ Trouble with interpersonal decision-making

▶ Tearfulness, increased likelihood of becoming emotionally upset

▶ Appetite changes

▶ Social withdrawal

▶ Executive functioning difficulties

▶ Fatigue

▶ Sense of emptiness

AUTISTIC BURNOUT

▶ **LOSS OF ABILITY TO MASK:** *Often leads to the person appearing "more Autistic" during burnout*

▶ **BENEFITS FROM REST AND UNMASKING:** *Can be alleviated by self-care, sensory relief, unmasking, and engaging in personal interests*

▶ **WORSENS WITH BEHAVIORAL ACTIVATION:** *Burnout exacerbated by excessive activity*

▶ **SENSORY SENSITIVITIES:** *Increased sensitivities to stimuli*

▶ **LOSS OF SKILLS:** *Decline in executive function, communication, and life skills*

▶ **NONEXISTENCE IDEATION:** *A longing for demands and sensory input to stop, sometimes leading to daydreams of nonexistence (a desire to not exist, or just wanting all the demands to stop, but not an active desire to unalive oneself)*

The Challenge in Recognizing the Signs of Autistic Burnout

Recognizing the early signs of burnout is essential for effective management and prevention. These initial indicators serve as critical feedback from your system, signaling that it's time to slow down and prioritize self-care.

Over the next several pages, we'll dive into the various signs and symptoms of burnout, starting with a comprehensive overview of the most common experiences. Then you'll find a checklist so you can track your own signs and symptoms. The checklist outlines the three primary symptom clusters of burnout: pervasive exhaustion, heightened sensory sensitivities, and loss of skills.

Identifying burnout can be challenging for two main reasons:

1 **Many adults don't realize they are Autistic until they're already experiencing significant burnout.** In some cases, burnout precipitates the diagnosis of autism, as Autistic traits become more pronounced and the ability to mask diminishes. This explains why burnout can be so hard to detect and why many people go through such severe burnout phases.

2 **The complexities of masking, people-pleasing behaviors, and interoception difficulties are significant obstacles to identifying your signs and symptoms.** Despite these challenges, you *can* become more adept at identifying personal burnout signs and taking timely action, therefore minimizing prolonged deep burnout periods.

Armed with this knowledge, you'll be equipped to draft a personalized plan, pinpointing the early signs and symptoms that indicate the onset of burnout for you, laying the foundation for proactive burnout management and recovery strategies.

Barriers to Early Identification of Burnout

Many Autistic people don't immediately recognize the signs and symptoms of burnout, thanks to three main factors: interoception struggles, masking, and people-pleasing tendencies. After each section, jot down a note about your experiences with each factor.

INTEROCEPTION STRUGGLES

Interoceptive awareness is the ability to perceive, identify, and understand what's happening inside your body, such as the urge to urinate or eliminate, the sense of fullness or hunger, cramps, thirst, pain, tension, emotions, or fatigue. When this sense isn't as sharp, it can be harder to notice the subtle changes that signal burnout, like increased fatigue or emotional exhaustion. Many people with interoception challenges won't be getting the signals from their bodies that it's time to slow down, so they won't notice signs of burnout until they have overdone it.

MASKING

Masking complicates self-awareness by requiring you to interpret others' nonverbal cues with heightened sensitivity, while simultaneously suppressing your natural instincts for self-soothing. You therefore minimize and discredit your bodily signals, while instead being hypervigilant toward external cues. This pattern of ignoring personal needs in an effort to conform can cause you to lose touch with your needs, potentially overlooking your body's early signs of illness or burnout.

PEOPLE-PLEASING

If you engage in people-pleasing or are inclined toward a fawn response—which is the process of trying to appease a threat—you may find it difficult to notice signs of burnout. Neglecting oneself in the pursuit of acceptance or safety is more prevalent in Autistic people.

Common Autistic Burnout Symptoms

Experiencing Autistic burnout means your nervous system is in a state of burnout. So, many of the "symptoms" of Autistic burnout, such as an increased need for routine, are actually you leveraging coping strategies to regulate an overwhelmed nervous system. This is because Autistic people have a unique nervous system—a topic we'll explore in greater detail in Chapter 4.

Following is a list of common manifestations, though it's not all-encompassing. It's important to assess these symptoms against your personal baseline, because certain challenges, like difficulty adapting to change, are universal among Autistic people but intensify during burnout.

▶ Enhanced difficulty managing emotions, leading to more frequent outbursts, intense anxiety, and mood swings

▶ An increase in Autistic traits, such as repetitive behaviors and a stronger need for routine

▶ A greater need for stimming (sensory-based self-soothing behaviors)

▶ Increased difficulty with adapting to change or transitioning between tasks and activities

▶ Impaired executive functioning skills, evident in challenges with planning, organization, and decision-making

▶ Sensory overload, prompting either sensory seeking or sensory avoidance behaviors

▶ Cognitive fatigue, marked by slower thought processes, trouble finding words, and memory issues

▶ Social challenges, including more pronounced difficulties with social interactions, communication, and making eye contact

▶ Increased sensitivity to everyday noises, smells, sights, and sensations

▶ Avoidance of social situations and interactions stemming from overwhelming social fatigue

▶ Decreased tolerance for certain foods

▶ Loss or deterioration of skills related to work

How to Use the Autistic Burnout Checklist

The following pages provide a checklist of common Autistic burnout symptoms, divided into three main symptom clusters:

 **SYMPTOM CLUSTER A**	**SYMPTOM CLUSTER B**	**SYMPTOM CLUSTER C**
Pervasive physical, emotional, and cognitive exhaustion	*An increase in sensory sensitivities*	*Loss of skills*

You can fill out the next three pages now, then return here to tally your total score. As you work your way through the book, it can be beneficial to redo this checklist as you make progress in your recovery. Additionally, keep in mind that your experiences may be unique and go beyond what's covered in this checklist. Feel free to create your own checklist or "litmus test" to gauge the extent of your burnout.

Note: Many of the items on this checklist will feel relatable because you're Autistic. To get the most accurate results, compare each item to your baseline. For example, if the checklist says "I struggle to plan my day," check it off only if this feels noticeably different or more difficult than usual.

TOTAL SCORE

SYMPTOM CLUSTER A	Total Score ➡	**/18**
SYMPTOM CLUSTER B	Total Score ➡	**/18**
SYMPTOM CLUSTER C	Total Score ➡	**/18**

TOTAL SCORE ➡ **/54**

 DISCLAIMER: *This is not an official assessment or screener; rather, it is a compilation of common symptoms of burnout across various domains. Please view this as one data point and take into account other medical conditions that may affect your responses to these questions.*

This checklist draws inspiration from Dr. Alice Nicholls's ABSC Checklist (available at https://dralicenicholls.com/wp-content/uploads/2021/09/The-Autistic-Burnout-Symptom-Checklist-ABSC.pdf) and has been adapted to complement Dr. Dora Raymaker's burnout framework.

TRACK YOUR SYMPTOMS: **Exhaustion**

SYMPTOM CLUSTER A: *Pervasive Physical, Emotional, and Cognitive Exhaustion*

PHYSICAL EXHAUSTION

○ I feel run-down and drained of physical energy.
○ I am tired all the time and feel I need to sleep more.
○ I no longer have energy to engage my interests.
○ When I wake up in the morning, I still feel tired.
○ I feel as if I am running on empty all day long!
○ I spend most of my free time in bed or on the couch.

TOTAL SCORE ➡ /6

EMOTIONAL EXHAUSTION

○ I find it harder than usual to manage my emotions.
○ My emotions overwhelm me more easily.
○ I become more irritable and have a shorter fuse.
○ I am more tearful (or more emotionally numb and disconnected).
○ I find myself being harder on and less empathetic with people.
○ My emotions seem all over the place (more than usual).

TOTAL SCORE ➡ /6

COGNITIVE EXHAUSTION

○ Focusing on tasks feels really difficult.
○ I've noticed a loss or deterioration of my cognitive skills.
○ I feel mentally exhausted and find it challenging to think clearly.
○ My thinking is slowed down and foggy.
○ I am experiencing memory problems.
○ I'm having more difficulty understanding directions.

TOTAL SCORE ➡ /6

Total Cluster A Score ➡ /18

TRACK YOUR SYMPTOMS: Sensory Sensitivities

SYMPTOM CLUSTER B: *An Increase in Sensory Sensitivities*

HEIGHTENED SENSORY SENSITIVITIES

- ○ Weather changes impact me more noticeably now.
- ○ Previously ignorable sounds and smells now bother me.
- ○ I find it harder to tolerate physical touch from others.
- ○ I am more easily overwhelmed by bright lights or busy environments.
- ○ I'm more sensitive to feelings of hunger or fullness.
- ○ My diet has narrowed as tastes and textures bother me more.

TOTAL SCORE ➔ /6

SENSORY REGULATION DIFFICULTIES

- ○ I am experiencing more frequent sensory meltdowns.
- ○ I am experiencing more frequent sensory shutdowns.
- ○ I engage in more stimming (sensory-input-seeking behavior).
- ○ I rely more on sensory tools like fidget toys.
- ○ The intensity of my sensory meltdowns/shutdowns has increased.
- ○ I have more difficulty filtering out irrelevant sensory information.

TOTAL SCORE ➔ /6

ROUTINE DISRUPTIONS

- ○ I need more time to mentally prepare for transitions in activities.
- ○ I find it harder to start planned activities.
- ○ Shifting from one task to another has become increasingly difficult.
- ○ Unexpected changes in my daily schedule throw me off-balance.
- ○ I'm sticking to my routines more strictly than usual.
- ○ Spontaneous events feel overwhelming, even if they're minor.

TOTAL SCORE ➔ /6

Total Cluster B Score ➔ /18

TRACK YOUR SYMPTOMS: Loss of Skills

SYMPTOM CLUSTER C: *Loss of Skills*

EXECUTIVE FUNCTIONING (EF)

- ○ I struggle to plan my day.
- ○ Tasks that were once manageable now seem overwhelming.
- ○ I have difficulty starting tasks or switching between tasks.
- ○ I find it hard to make decisions.
- ○ I have decreased ability to solve problems.
- ○ I am having increased difficulty with organization.

TOTAL SCORE ➡ **/6**

COMMUNICATION SKILLS

- ○ I find it hard to find the right words.
- ○ I have more difficulty processing what people are saying.
- ○ I have a diminished capacity for small talk.
- ○ I seem to have less capacity to socialize.
- ○ Talking to people feels like too much effort.
- ○ It takes me longer to respond to people.

TOTAL SCORE ➡ **/6**

LIFE SKILLS

- ○ I find it challenging to manage daily routines.
- ○ I struggle with personal hygiene (e.g., showering, brushing teeth).
- ○ I have difficulty managing my medication and healthcare routines.
- ○ I have difficulty with cooking, preparing, or eating meals.
- ○ I find it hard to maintain my living space.
- ○ I have difficulty with transportation or navigating public spaces.

TOTAL SCORE ➡ **/6**

Total Cluster C Score ➡ **/18**

Autistic Burnout Signs, in Our Own Words

The checklists on the previous pages sum up common signs and symptoms. Here are some additional signs that people in my community mentioned:

"My creativity goes away. I stop making art and putting thought into my appearance."

"My brain fog increases, and my access to language and words goes away."

"Projects I was so excited about now feel like mountains. I can't do small daily things that felt simple before. I feel behind on everything and have no desire to catch up."

"When I'm not in burnout, I can sit in a coffee shop and see beauty in the people around me interacting, enjoying one another, connecting. In burnout, I look at them and am abhorred. I don't have tolerance for humanity."

"It's harder to smile, like my cheeks legit feel too heavy to raise into a smile."

"I experience skill regression and find it difficult to coordinate, balance, and articulate my body. I have difficulty walking in a straight line, I struggle to stand upright without falling, I drop things, and I bump into things."

"My body is very heavy. I can't move. Sensory sensitivities, especially sound, are next level. I rock a lot more."

"During Autistic burnout I experience regular suicidal ideation that is totally unlike my past experiences with depression—I am operating so far beyond my actual capacity that I just can't fathom the thought of pushing my brain and body to do one more thing."

"I daydream more (about escape, having no demands, etc.)."

"My special interests stop providing me comfort, and I start pulling away from people and isolating."

"The endless number of systems I have in place to cope with being an AuDHDer (person with autism and ADHD) start to fail, and I start to make little mistakes or forget things."

★ ★ ★
EXAMPLE

Map Out Your Burnout Signs

These pages provide a more visual way to capture your signs and symptoms.

MY BODY FEELS	EMOTIONS	COGNITIVE/EF SKILLS
▶ *Pain tolerance lower* ▶ *Slow* ▶ *Foggy* ▶ *Heavy*	▶ *Heightened emotions (more irritable)* ▶ *Patience declines, more easily agitated*	▶ *More forgetful* ▶ *Difficulty focusing* ▶ *More difficulty organizing and breaking down tasks* ▶ *Difficulty starting tasks*

SENSORY SENSITIVITIES	SENSORY OVERWHELM	SENSORY ROUTINES
▶ *Sounds more abrasive* ▶ *Less tolerance for busy environments* ▶ *Rely more on safe foods*	▶ *An increase in sensory shutdowns* ▶ *More stimming* ▶ *Crave more deep pressure*	▶ *More difficulty with transitions* ▶ *Increased irritability with change*

INTEREST/MOTIVATION	COMMUNICATION	LIFE SKILLS
▶ *Less motivation to engage in my special interests* ▶ *Loss of energy or motivation to do the things I want to do*	▶ *Difficulty finding words* ▶ *Reduced ability for small talk*	▶ *Difficulty with basic self-care (grooming, showering, medication)*

Map Out Your Burnout Signs

MY BODY FEELS	EMOTIONS	COGNITIVE/EF SKILLS

SENSORY SENSITIVITIES	SENSORY OVERWHELM	SENSORY ROUTINES

INTEREST/MOTIVATION	COMMUNICATION	LIFE SKILLS

FILL IN YOUR OWN!

What are other distinct signs, perhaps related to sleep, food, body coordination, or relationships changes?

External Markers
OF AUTISTIC BURNOUT

Even with the Autistic Burnout Checklist, it might be difficult for you to spot the signs of burnout. If so, you can cultivate this awareness through techniques like regular self-reflections, reconnecting with bodily sensations through specific practices, or leaning on supportive individuals who recognize your distinct signs of burnout.

Another helpful strategy is to distinguish between burnout's external and internal signs. If you have interoception challenges, external indicators—observable behaviors and changes—are often easier to identify. The upcoming pages include examples of these markers and a space to write in your own markers.

External burnout markers may include:

- *Difficulty speaking or articulating thoughts*

- *Increase in errors*

- *Increased tearfulness and emotional responses*

- *Frequent meltdowns or shutdowns*

- *Altered eating habits*

- *Social withdrawal*

- *Physical symptoms of stress*

- *Decline in performance*

- *Reduced engagement in personal interests*

- *Struggling with initiation*

- *Increase in substance use*

What Are Your External Markers?

Write down any external signs of burnout that you experience.

Internal Markers
OF AUTISTIC BURNOUT

Internal markers of burnout are more about personal feelings and internal experiences, which might not be immediately visible to others but are deeply felt by you:

- *Persistent fatigue or exhaustion*
- *Feeling overwhelmed or hopeless*
- *Decreased satisfaction or fulfillment*
- *Emotional numbness or detachment*
- *Anxiety or increased worry*
- *Difficulty concentrating or indecisiveness*
- *Sense of ineffectiveness or lack of accomplishment*
- *Irritability or a short temper*
- *Physical symptoms of stress*
- *Nonexistence fantasies (distinct from suicidal ideation)*

What Are Your Internal Markers?

Write down any internal signs of burnout that you experience.

Causes of Autistic Burnout

Autistic burnout creeps up when the demands of living in a predominantly allistic world pile up beyond our capacity to cope. It's particularly prevalent among those of us who expend significant energy camouflaging and masking to fit into social molds. But it's not just caused by social gymnastics; it's also a result of:

- Wrestling with the expectations of a neurotypical world that doesn't quite see you

- The frustrating gap in autism awareness that can lead to being misunderstood, misdiagnosed, or left without support

- The constant barrage of sensory input that demands your attention

- The tireless effort required for tasks that demand executive functioning

- The wear and tear of chronic stress

- The additional layer of navigating co-occurring mental and physical health issues

- The seismic shifts of life's transitions, whether it's puberty, moving into adulthood, or other major life stages or changes

- The challenge of understanding your own emotions and bodily signals, thanks to alexithymia and issues with interoception

Fully understanding Autistic burnout means recognizing this tangled web of causes and contributors. Societal changes such as creating more sensory-friendly environments and promoting flexible work arrangements could help foster a world where Autistic people could thrive without the constant threat of burnout looming over us.

Dr. Dora Raymaker and their colleagues peeled back the layers of what causes Autistic burnout in their landmark 2020 study. They frame it as the result of life's pressures accumulating beyond what a person can handle, especially when finding support feels like navigating a labyrinth. A simplified equation looks something like this:

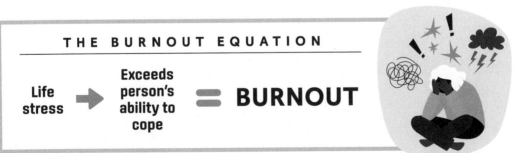

THE BURNOUT EQUATION

Life stress → **Exceeds person's ability to cope** = **BURNOUT**

Alexithymia and atypical interoception

Navigating the expectations of a neurotypical world

Life transitions such as puberty, transition to adulthood, and menopause

VISUALIZING THE CAUSES OF
AUTISTIC BURNOUT

Masking and camouflaging

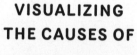

Sensory overwhelm

Co-occurring medical or mental health conditions

Lack of accommodations and difficulty accessing informed healthcare

Experiencing stigma, discrimination, or victimization

When Your Bucket Overflows

Many Autistic people experience their first burnout during adolescence. Burnout might continue to occur until you make significant lifestyle adjustments to more sustainably balance demands. This workbook is crafted to guide you through that process. As someone who thinks visually, I find it helpful to picture the autism burnout equation (where life's stress surpasses your coping abilities) using a simple metaphor: Envision a running faucet representing stress and demands, and a container symbolizing your capacity to cope.

If the faucet's flow is strong, it quickly fills any container, regardless of its sturdiness or size. And if your container is as small as a miniature teacup, it's bound to overflow in no time.

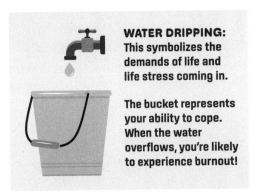

WATER DRIPPING: This symbolizes the demands of life and life stress coming in.

The bucket represents your ability to cope. When the water overflows, you're likely to experience burnout!

In order to craft a manageable life, it's important to address two key aspects:

1 Reducing the faucet's flow

2 Enlarging your container's capacity

Chapter 2 dives deeper into this framework and is followed by chapters designed to both expand your bucket and reduce the flow of the faucet:

CHAPTER 3 on sensory regulation focuses on diminishing the "faucet" of sensory overload. Interestingly, by achieving sensory regulation, you can also increase your "container's" size, addressing both sides of the equation.

CHAPTER 4 on nervous system regulation concentrates on enlarging your "container" (supporting your nervous system) to enhance your ability to handle stressors.

CHAPTERS 5 AND 6, dedicated to energy management and sleep, suggest ideas to further expand your coping capacity.

CHAPTERS 7 AND 8, focusing on masking and the practice of setting boundaries and accommodations, are about turning down the "faucet"—reducing demands by masking less, establishing more accommodations, and maintaining healthy boundaries.

CHAPTER 2

Building an Autistic Burnout Recovery Plan

How to Approach Recovery

I wish I could hand you a miraculous, quick-fix solution that promises a full recovery from Autistic burnout in a matter of weeks. Unfortunately, that's not possible. Burnout accumulates over years of sensory overload, nervous system dysregulation, and the constant push beyond your limits. Consequently, the path to recovery is gradual and requires patience and persistence. One approach that can help is creating what I call an Autistic Burnout Recovery Plan, which is a collection of personalized strategies that can help you recover, recharge, and rebalance yourself.

Remember the faucet and bucket analogy from the end of Chapter 1? This chapter focuses on two key strategies for recovery:

1 Reducing your stress levels (turning down the faucet)

2 Increasing your coping capacity (expanding the bucket)

Following are some general things to keep in mind as you approach recovery.

Sometimes Less Is More

This chapter is packed with ideas—but please don't feel pressured to adopt them all! Explore the suggestions that resonate with you and set aside the rest for now.

Recovery Takes Time

There are no shortcuts in overcoming burnout, especially when you're balancing the demands of parenting, work, school, or managing health conditions. One of the most critical steps in recovering from Autistic burnout is cultivating patience—toward yourself and the recovery process. Approach this journey with kindness, gentleness, and understanding.

Recovery Is Very Personal

Recovery from Autistic burnout is deeply personal. That's why this book allows you to consider and record what works best for *you*. For some, it involves embracing rest and prioritizing sleep, while others may focus on healing trauma and attachment wounds. On a larger scale, recovery might mean a comprehensive lifestyle revision, reevaluating your relationships with food, alcohol, health, exercise, sleep, work, and sensory environments. These are profound and individual transformations that will involve your creativity, dedication, and time.

Acknowledging Privilege and Systemic Inequality

It's essential to recognize the presence of privilege in conversations about self-care and manageable demands. Discussions about reducing demands can inadvertently disregard the reality that **not everyone enjoys the same privileges**. For example, Black, Brown, and trans Autistic people often lack the safety to unmask, and single-parent households or people facing financial hardships may not have the privilege of easily reducing their demands.

Likewise, it's important to recognize that burnout occurs within a systemic context. And **our systemic context happens to be one that is racist, homophobic, and transphobic and disproportionately impacts disabled people**.

Therefore, we'll take a balanced approach here, acknowledging systemic injustices beyond your direct control while focusing on the aspects you may have some influence over. The following exercise will help you distinguish between the things you're concerned about but can't control and the things you can actually influence. While it's natural to care about many things, focusing too much on what's outside your control can lead to a greater sense of disempowerment. By identifying where you have influence, you can channel your energy more effectively and tap into a sense of agency.

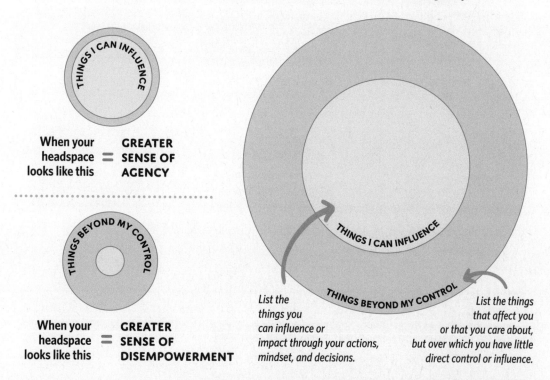

THINGS I CAN INFLUENCE

When your headspace looks like this = GREATER SENSE OF AGENCY

THINGS BEYOND MY CONTROL

When your headspace looks like this = GREATER SENSE OF DISEMPOWERMENT

THINGS I CAN INFLUENCE

THINGS BEYOND MY CONTROL

List the things you can influence or impact through your actions, mindset, and decisions.

List the things that affect you or that you care about, but over which you have little direct control or influence.

Turn Down Your Faucet

WATER DRIPPING: This symbolizes the demands of life and life stress coming in.

The bucket represents your ability to cope. When the water overflows, you're likely to experience burnout!

To address burnout, one of the main strategies we'll work on in this chapter is reducing the inflow of demands, stressors, and pressures. This page outlines some key ways to do that. The following pages will then explain each one in more detail.

Seek Social Support

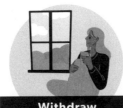

Withdraw Strategically When Necessary

Drop Unnecessary Demands

Outsource Mindfully

Practice Good Boundaries

Reduce Your Sensory Load

Find Formal Supports

Simplify Your Routine

Unmask When Possible

Seek Social Support

Here are some examples of ways to draw on your support network to turn down the faucet.

DELEGATE TASKS

Do you have a support network that would be willing to help you out with some tasks? When possible, delegate some responsibilities to others, whether at work or home. Jot down here some tasks you might be able to delegate.

✎

CONSIDER ALTERNATIVE COMMUNICATION

If you typically interact in person with friends or family, ask them if they'd be willing to engage with you via text or digital correspondence. This can provide a more comfortable and manageable way to stay connected. Are there any in-person interactions that you'd like to move to digital? Write them down here.

✎

COMMUNICATE YOUR LIMITS

Let your friends and family know that your ability to socialize is currently limited. Express your appreciation for their understanding and let them know that, even though you may not have the capacity for deep engagement right now, their presence means a lot to you. Sometimes, simply knowing that a friend doesn't have an expectation for you to return their text can go a long way in reducing stress. In the space here, brainstorm a quick message you could share with people to convey this message. For example, you could copy and paste a text response or set up an automated email responder that says something like this: "Thanks for writing. I'm working on maintaining a healthier digital balance, so it may take me a bit of time to respond."

✎

Withdraw Strategically When Necessary

While withdrawal is commonly linked to depression and adverse consequences, within the context of burnout, it can serve as a useful method to regulate energy, address sensory needs, and proactively prevent burnout.

CANCEL NONESSENTIAL COMMITMENTS

Evaluate your calendar and cancel nonessential appointments or commitments. In the space here, write down a few one-time or ongoing commitments that you might be able to cancel.

LIMIT SMALL TALK

Engaging in small talk can be especially challenging during burnout. Consider developing a brief script to politely navigate away from small talk situations. For example, you might say something like, "It was great chatting with you. I need to step away now, but have a wonderful day!" Use the space here to brainstorm a script that could work for you.

REDUCE YOUR WORKLOAD

Delegate tasks at work or temporarily reduce work hours; consider taking paid time off or disability leave if accessible. Write down work tasks that you could consider asking to be taken off your plate.

SOCIALIZE SELECTIVELY

Be mindful of social engagements. Say yes to high-value activities and drop the rest. Jot down here some people you'd like to prioritize seeing.

Drop Unnecessary Demands

Knowing which demands can be dropped and which are nonnegotiable is crucial. Here are some examples of ways to reduce the number of demands on your time and energy. Your goal is to streamline and simplify, because doing less will help you manage your task load to help avoid burnout. Here are some examples.

SIMPLIFY YOUR MEALS: Explore simple and quick meal options that reduce the demand of cooking complex dishes. This could include grab-and-go salads, frozen meals, sandwiches, or one-pot recipes. Write down some ideas that could make your meal planning or preparation easier.

AUTOMATE TASKS: Use technology and automation tools to handle repetitive tasks. For example, set up automatic bill payments or use grocery-delivery services. Come up with some tasks you could automate here.

OUTSOURCE MINDFULLY: Explore outsourcing options for tasks that you find particularly draining or challenging. We'll talk more about this topic on the next page.

THINK OF WHAT TO SAY AHEAD OF TIME: Practice politely declining additional commitments or requests that aren't essential at the moment. That way, when you're put on the spot, you have some phrasing in mind already. You don't need to offer an excuse; you can just say something like, "I love this event, but unfortunately I can't help with it this year." Write down some ways of saying no that feel natural to you.

PRACTICE SELF-COMPASSION: Be gentle with yourself and acknowledge that it's okay to drop certain demands temporarily. One way to do that is to talk to yourself like you'd talk to a friend. Write down some statements here that will help you internalize self-compassion. For example, "It's okay to let go of some tasks for now."

Outsource Mindfully

If you find yourself in a position to outsource tasks, now is an opportune moment to do so. If you have the budget, consider paying a company to take on tasks for you. If not, you might reach out to your social support network to explore potential tasks that can be delegated to alleviate some of your demands.

HOUSE CLEANING

Ease your load by hiring someone to assist with household cleaning tasks. Which tasks would you most like to take off your plate? Write them down here.

FOOD SERVICES

Explore various options, such as stocking up on safe frozen foods (mine are frozen burritos), subscribing to a meal-delivery service, or trying a grocery store that delivers. Jot down some ideas related to food that you could outsource.

CHILDCARE

If you are a parent, you have additional demands. Even if it's just for a few hours of much-needed demand-free time, consider hiring childcare. Try to think of any nearby people or services you could use for this task and write them down here.

VIRTUAL ASSISTANT

Consider hiring a virtual assistant to help with administrative tasks, email management, and scheduling, freeing up your time for essential activities. What responsibilities could this person easily help you with? You can keep a running list here.

Practice Good Boundaries

Boundaries are difficult for a lot of Autistic people, but they become essential when you're working to turn down the faucet. Because knowing how to say no can be hard, here are a few examples of ways to do so.

Some Ways of Saying No . . .

Pro tip: Keep it simple. You don't owe anyone a detailed explanation for why you're declining. While explaining your burnout may be important in some contexts, it can also be energy consuming. It's perfectly acceptable to politely state that you're unable to do something at the moment. For example:

> ▶ *I am sorry; I can't do that right now.*
> ▶ *I have to pass on this one, but I appreciate your understanding.*
> ▶ *Unfortunately, I don't have the bandwidth for that right now.*
> ▶ *I'm honored you asked me, but I simply can't.*
> ▶ *I'm currently focusing on other priorities.*
> ▶ *I wish I were able to. I'm afraid I can't.*

Now take a moment to write a couple of options that feel right to you. Go ahead and adjust or combine any of the examples on this page or start from scratch. You can also practice saying your responses aloud in a mirror to get yourself more comfortable with the words and the process.

Reduce Your Sensory Load

To turn down the pace of your faucet, you can also make sensory adjustments: Swap out bright light fixtures, create a sensory-detox space, use sensory tools like weighted blankets or noise blockers, and remove irritants like perfumes and chemical smells from your living space. These seemingly small changes can make a big difference. In burnout, your sensory system is heightened, so reducing unnecessary sensory input is important.

SENSORY DETOX

Allocate dedicated quiet time and sensory-detox periods. Many Autistic people find it essential to be physically alone to achieve full relaxation. How do you like to detox from sensory input? Reflect on your preferences here.

LIMIT SENSORY INPUT

Create a sensory-friendly environment by reducing noise, lights, or other sensory triggers. Identify sensory irritants like perfumes or other chemicals in your home. In the space provided, track the inputs that tend to bother you when you feel burned out.

USE SENSORY BLOCKERS

Use sensory blockers like sunglasses, sound blockers, or compression clothing to reduce sensory input when navigating high-sensory environments. Jot down here the blockers you prefer.

REVISIT YOUR HYGIENE ROUTINES

Consider quick swaps that might help reduce overload. Can you reduce the frequency of showers or replace them with dry shampoo and wipes? Reflect on grooming activities that may trigger sensory overload and think about alternatives or ways to simplify them in the space here.

Find Formal Supports

One of the primary reasons your stress faucet may be running at full blast is the absence of formal accommodations. Without these accommodations, you likely find yourself working harder to compensate. Implementing accommodations is a highly effective way to slow down the stress faucet and create a more manageable environment.

While you can always self-advocate and ask for accommodations, the accessibility of certain formal accommodations may vary depending on your diagnosis status.

Some Accommodations That May Be Available to You

In the space provided, write down personalized notes that capture how each particular accommodation could potentially work for you.

FLEXIBLE WORK HOURS: Adjust your work hours to better suit your energy levels and sensory needs.

ACCOMMODATIONS FOR MEETINGS: Seek accommodations for meetings, such as shorter durations or virtual attendance options.

REMOTE WORK: The option to work from home or a quieter environment can provide relief from sensory overload.

ACADEMIC ACCOMMODATIONS: You may be eligible for academic accommodations at your educational institution. This could include extended test-taking time, note-taking support, or access to assistive technology.

SENSORY BREAKS: Schedule regular sensory breaks during your school or work day.

COMMUNICATION PREFERENCES: Do you prefer multiple forms of communication? Specify your preferred communication methods, such as email or messaging apps.

Simplify Your Routine

When you're in burnout, it's tempting to let your routine go. But it's important to not let your routine go, because routines are soothing to your nervous system—they tell you what to expect. Your routine doesn't have to be rigorous, but it is helpful to have a few anchor points during the day. So, simplify your daily routine to minimize decision-making and mental fatigue!

CREATE A MINIMALIST ROUTINE

In the space here, design a simplified daily routine with a minimal number of tasks. Stick to the basics like self-care, work, and rest.

USE VISUAL REMINDERS AND PROMPTS

Visual cues or reminders, such as sticky notes, smartphone alarms, or apps, can help prompt you to remember essential tasks without relying on memory alone. When in burnout, you might benefit from prompts to get you going. Jot down some reminders that might work for you.

TIME BLOCKING

Allocate specific time blocks for different activities. This can help you stay organized and prevent feeling overwhelmed by multitasking. Break down your day into a few chunks in the space here.

SCHEDULE STRUCTURED DOWNTIME

Don't forget to schedule structured downtime and time with your interests and energy sparks! Make a list here of things you love to do in your downtime.

Unmask When Possible

Masking is one of the drivers of burnout because it requires a lot of cognitive energy! So, one way of reducing the flow of your faucet is to spend less time masking. Here are a few considerations.

UNMASK IN PRIVATE

Masking is usually not a conscious decision. Therefore, unmasking is often a journey of self-discovery, where you learn about your likes, preferences, and soothing movements. Take time to practice in private, experiment with movements and stimming, and explore your personal preferences. Write down what you learn about your preferences here.

SENSORY PLAY

Play is a powerful way to reconnect with your preferences and rediscover your authentic self. Dedicate time to play. If play feels unfamiliar, reflect on how you played as a child as a way to reconnect with your inner child. Make a quick list here of ways you like to play.

LIMIT TIME IN MASKING SPACES

Whenever possible, minimize the amount of time you spend in social environments where you feel compelled to mask. Can you think of particular high-masking events that you could pull back from?

FIND YOUR SAFE PEOPLE

Identify the people in your life with whom you feel safe and comfortable, and intentionally spend time with them to practice unmasking. Write down your safe people here.

★ ★ ★
EXAMPLE

At-a-Glance Ways to Turn Down Your Faucet

SEEK SOCIAL SUPPORT	WITHDRAW STRATEGICALLY WHEN NECESSARY	DROP UNNECESSARY DEMANDS
▶ *Ask my mom to watch the kids once a week* ▶ *Discuss with my partner about primarily communicating via text instead of spoken conversations*	▶ *Focus on high-value social interactions and politely decline others for now* ▶ *Avoid high-sensory events to manage sensory overload*	▶ *Be selective about medical appointments and social commitments*

OUTSOURCE MINDFULLY	PRACTICE GOOD BOUNDARIES	REDUCE YOUR SENSORY LOAD
▶ *Order groceries for delivery* ▶ *Utilize meal services or order food online for at least three meals a week*	▶ *Practice saying no once this week*	▶ *Use ear blockers or loops as needed* ▶ *Create a sensory soothing kit for stressful times*

FIND FORMAL SUPPORTS	SIMPLIFY YOUR ROUTINE	UNMASK WHEN POSSIBLE
▶ *Talk to my employer about potential accommodations*	▶ *Streamline my morning routine for a smoother start to the day* ▶ *Include time for engaging with interests and rest in my daily routine*	▶ *Explore enjoyable forms of movement and stimming in private* ▶ *Identify people in my life with whom it is safe to be myself*

At-a-Glance Ways to Turn Down Your Faucet

SEEK SOCIAL SUPPORT	WITHDRAW STRATEGICALLY WHEN NECESSARY	DROP UNNECESSARY DEMANDS
OUTSOURCE MINDFULLY	**PRACTICE GOOD BOUNDARIES**	**REDUCE YOUR SENSORY LOAD**
FIND FORMAL SUPPORTS	SIMPLIFY YOUR ROUTINE	UNMASK WHEN POSSIBLE
CREATE YOUR OWN!		

Expand Your Bucket

Consider What Works for You

When exploring different techniques to expand your bucket, keep in mind that what works for you will not necessarily be the same as what works for others. One person might benefit a lot from managing their nervous system, while another sees great results when they exercise. It's a very individual process, and that's why the following pages will encourage you to reflect on what works best for *you*.

There's No Need to Try Everything at Once

When looking at all the suggestions on the upcoming pages, it is easy to become overwhelmed, particularly if you think you need to incorporate all of them at once. Instead, try focusing on just one at a time. The beauty is that even addressing one aspect will expand your capacity, potentially making it easier to tackle others.

Where Should You Start?

In deciding where to start, I recommend one of two approaches:

1 Start with the area that needs the most attention. For example, if sleep is a challenge for you, you might consider starting there.

2 Start with an area that you are excited about or that feels the easiest to address. For example, if connection is particularly motivating for you, beginning with a focus on belonging could be a good choice.

Effective Ways to Expand Your Bucket

Manage Your Energy

Focus on Belonging and Support

Adjust Your Lifestyle

Prioritize and Improve Your Sleep

Practice Self-Advocacy

Lean Into Your Autistic Strengths

Look for Self-Insight

Regulate Your Nervous System

Consider Psychological and Mindset Work

Manage Your Energy

A key component of expanding your bucket's capacity is learning how to work with your energy rather than against it. Employing pacing systems, spending time doing things that spark energy, and increasing insight into your energy can go a long way.

PACE YOURSELF

Pacing systems are helpful tools for managing energy intentionally and are commonly used within disability spaces. Pacing systems can help you track your energy and intentionally build in rest between high-energy tasks—you'll learn much more about them in Chapter 5. For now, just write down the pacing systems you've heard of, if any.

✎

FIND YOUR ENERGY SPARKS

Energy sparks are those activities that give you energy, such as immersing yourself in personal interests or embarking on creative projects. As you navigate the process of conserving energy, it's equally important to schedule activities that ignite your energy levels. Make a list of some of your energy sparks here.

✎

CULTIVATE ENERGY EFFICIENCY

Developing efficiency in your daily activities can significantly impact your energy management. Explore ways to streamline tasks, minimize unnecessary energy expenditure, and optimize your routines for greater energy conservation. This may involve incorporating some executive functioning supports into your life! Can you think of any ways to become more efficient?

✎

INCORPORATE RESTORATIVE MOMENTS

Incorporate restful moments throughout your day. Short breaks for relaxation exercises, deep breathing, or a brief walk can help replenish your energy reserves. Opt for activities that offer genuine restoration rather than quick fixes that don't deeply rejuvenate you. Examples of truly restorative rest include diving into a special interest, immersing yourself in nature, or engaging in soothing sensory activities. Which areas of your day need a restful moment? Write them here.

✎

Focus on Belonging and Support

Belonging and social support have consistently been identified as protective factors for wellness and mental health. But navigating social relationships is also precisely what is often hard for many of us! Embracing Autistic culture and connecting with people in ways that align with your natural inclinations can foster a sense of belonging.

ENGAGE WITH THE AUTISTIC COMMUNITY

Engaging with the Autistic community can be a powerful way to recognize and validate your experience of burnout. It provides an opportunity to connect with like-minded people, ensures that you feel welcomed in a space, and nurtures Autistic pride. Finding your neurokin allows you to connect with people who truly understand you and cultivates a sense of belonging. Write down any ways you do or would like to connect with the Autistic community.

EMBRACE ACCEPTANCE AND SEEK SOCIAL SUPPORT

Accepting your neurodivergent identity and seeking out social support are vital steps in your burnout-recovery journey. These steps include accessing individual and community support, engaging in peer support, attending to your Autistic needs, and dedicating time to unmasking. Do you feel you've accepted your neurodivergent identity, or are you still on that journey? Reflect on that topic here.

CONNECT IN WAYS THAT FEEL GOOD TO YOU

Autistic people often have distinct and meaningful ways of connecting with others. These connections may involve shared interests, parallel play, engagement in advocacy projects aligned with our values, and direct and deep communication. In what ways do you like to connect with others? Use the space here to reflect on and write down your preferred methods of connection.

Adjust Your Lifestyle

There are various lifestyle changes that can enhance nervous system and emotional resilience, ultimately expanding your capacity to handle stressors. However, it's important to recognize that some of these changes may be more challenging for Autistic people to implement, so be gentle with yourself. Take your time and be kind to yourself as you explore what works best for you.

MOVE YOUR BODY

Movement is incredibly beneficial for our bodies. It helps complete the stress cycle (see the Regulate Your Nervous System page in this chapter and more detail on this topic in Chapter 4) and increases vagal tone. The key is to find movement that is soothing for you. It doesn't have to be traditional exercise, which may be less accessible. Focus on gentle and soothing ways to move your body. Use the space here to write down some movement ideas that might be soothing for you.

✎

HYDRATE

This may sound simple, but staying properly hydrated can be a struggle, especially if you have difficulties with interoceptive awareness and don't receive clear thirst cues. When you are hydrated, you're more likely to experience improved cognitive function, better mood, more energy, and overall improved physical health. Write down one way you could increase your water intake (some examples: make it taste good by adding fruit slices for flavor, use electrolyte pills, or create a water goal with a large water bottle).

TRY TO MANAGE YOUR STRESS

Practices like deep breathing and sensory soothing activities, along with addressing cognitive distortions, play an important role in managing your stress. These methods help reduce your body's central stress response. Record any techniques you currently use to manage stress here.

KEEP AN EYE ON YOUR NUTRITION

Autistic people are often more susceptible to vitamin deficiencies, particularly when navigating limited diets due to sensory issues. Balancing safe foods with nutrient-dense foods to complement safe foods and using high-quality vitamin supplements are a few ways to support all that your body is doing.

Many Autistic people experience food intolerances and sensitivities that can impact our energy levels. Recognizing and managing these sensitivities, while also ensuring a balanced nutrient intake, can help improve overall health and energy. Take a moment to reflect on your current nutrition. Use the space here to reflect on one small way to boost your nutrition (e.g., adding one vegetable a day, incorporating a multivitamin, drinking a smoothie). Small changes compounded over time can make a big difference!

ADDRESS CO-OCCURRING MEDICAL CONDITIONS

Autistic people experience a higher likelihood of various medical conditions. Proactively seeking treatment and following treatment plans for these co-occurring conditions can help support your energy and overall well-being. Consulting with healthcare providers who have a deep understanding of autism can ensure you receive more tailored care. On a scale of 1–10, rate how well you are managing your co-occurring medical conditions. Are they well-managed, or is there room for improvement?

ADDRESS CO-OCCURRING MENTAL HEALTH CONDITIONS

Autistic people have an increased risk of experiencing mental health conditions such as depression, anxiety, and OCD. These mental health conditions can also increase the likelihood of burnout. Actively seeking treatment and following the prescribed guidelines for any mental health issues is key to building and maintaining your resilience. Take a moment to identify one small thing you could do to improve your management of a co-occurring mental health condition (e.g., scheduling therapy, creating a self-care routine, etc.).

Prioritize and Improve Your Sleep

Sleep is a critical factor in burnout recovery. Alongside consulting with your medical team to rule out any medical causes of sleep issues, here are some practices to improve your relationship with sleep! Check out Chapter 6 for more discussion of sleep.

ESTABLISH A SLEEP ROUTINE

A sleep routine is especially important for Autistic people, as many of us experience a flattened melatonin curve, potentially dulling the natural cues for sleep onset. A consistent routine aids in synchronizing your sleep-wake cycle and fortifying your circadian rhythm—another common challenge—thereby improving overall sleep quality. A sleep routine can include things like having a personalized self-care routine, reading or listening to an audiobook, doing some gentle stretches, using a specific essential oil, and more. What are some components of your routine, or components you want it to have? Jot them down here.

✎

REVIEW YOUR SLEEP HYGIENE

Sleep hygiene involves habits that enhance your sleep quality, such as sleeping in a dark, cool environment and reserving the bed exclusively for sleep (and intimacy). These habits foster a healthy connection between the bedroom and restful sleep. Write down what sleep hygiene practices are the most important for your sleep.

✎

PUT YOUR MIND TO SLEEP

Many of us have busy minds that get in the way of sleep. To quiet your mind, try a technique known as cognitive shuffling, which involves bringing to mind random, unrelated words or images to distract the mind. You can use apps like MySleepButton to give it a try. You'll also find a cognitive shuffling exercise in Chapter 6. What practices help you quiet your mind at night?

✎

Practice Self-Advocacy

Self-advocacy is vital for securing accommodations that can help you manage or limit burnout. By speaking up for your needs and getting the adjustments that work for you, you empower yourself on your path to healing and well-being.

GET CLEAR ON YOUR NEEDS

Identifying what accommodations you need is often the first step. Take time to observe your environment, pinpoint irritants, and consider what would support you. If recognizing your needs is challenging due to interoception difficulties, start by engaging in activities that enhance interoceptive awareness. Write down any accommodations you think you might need here.

MASTER SELF-ADVOCACY TOOLS

Self-advocacy isn't always an innate ability, but learning specific tips and practicing scripts can help you get better and better at it. Like any skill, self-advocacy requires practice and persistence to improve. Explore Chapter 8 for a range of self-advocacy resources. Reflect on your self-advocacy skills here. What are your strengths? Do you have any areas where you could improve?

SECURE NECESSARY ACCOMMODATIONS

Securing accommodations—whether formal or informal—can help ensure that your environment better meets your needs, reducing stress and exhaustion. Formal supports might include mental health services, time off, or other documented accommodations for work or school. This may require obtaining a formal autism diagnosis. Informal accommodations can involve using sensory supports like sunglasses, hats, or noise-blocking devices or giving yourself permission to socially disengage to manage sensory input. Use the space here to take stock of the formal and informal accommodations you currently have.

Lean Into Your Autistic Strengths

Leaning into your Autistic strengths—such as attention to detail, deep focus on interests, pattern recognition, and strong problem-solving skills—can expand your capabilities, resilience, and effectiveness. Recognizing and leaning into these strengths allows you to craft a life that supports your needs.

DRAW ON SPECIAL INTEREST ENERGY

Use your deep interests to find personal satisfaction and grow your expertise. Think about turning these passions into a career or finding roles that align with them. While it might not always be easy, doing what you love can bring more energy to your work life. Write down any passions you have that could be incorporated into a job.

LEVERAGE BOTTOM-UP PROCESSING

Bottom-up processing is a way of understanding information by starting with the details and building up to a complete picture. This kind of processing can be overwhelming and often means it takes longer to learn new systems and ideas. However, when you do learn something in this way, you understand it deeply. Leaning into this strength means giving yourself time to take in information and digest it, and reminding yourself that in the long run, this intensive way of understanding the world brings depth and complexity. Reflect on whether bottom-up processing resonates with you.

CELEBRATE YOUR VALUES

Many Autistic people have a strong sense of fairness and justice, which can be channeled into advocacy work or community engagement, fostering a sense of purpose and belonging. Living in alignment with your values can energize and motivate you. What values do you embrace that could be valuable in your community or the world at large? Write them down here.

Look for Self-Insight

A lack of self-insight and self-knowledge—along with alexithymia—could increase the likelihood that you'll experience burnout. Self-insight includes knowing your triggers, emotions, and what makes you tick. This page outlines some ways to practice self-insight.

BUILD INTEROCEPTIVE AWARENESS

Developing interoceptive awareness (body awareness) is key for understanding your needs, emotions, and sensory inputs. This awareness helps prevent burnout and increases resilience. Think about your interoceptive awareness levels and write down some notes about them here.

ADDRESS ALEXITHYMIA

Alexithymia, difficulty identifying or describing emotions, can increase the risk of burnout. However, it's possible to improve in this area with practice. There are various apps that can help with this, like How We Feel and other mood-tracking apps. What practices help you get in touch with your "inner world"—for example, journaling, mood trackers, an app, and/or therapy? Write them here.

PRACTICE EMOTIONAL EXPRESSION

For many Autistic people, traditional ways of showing feelings might not always align. You could try alternatives like writing, creating art, making collages, composing poems, or using music. Write down some emotional expression methods that work well for you.

IDENTIFY YOUR SENSORY NEEDS

Being aware of when you're experiencing sensory overload is key in allowing you to self-regulate and advocate for your needs. See Chapter 3 for more on this topic. Write down how you recognize when you're experiencing sensory overload.

Regulate Your Nervous System

Autistic people often have more sensitive nervous systems, making it easier to shift into a stress response, indicated by low vagal tone. Actively working to strengthen vagal tone and incorporating regular practices to support the nervous system can significantly increase your capacity to handle stress.

COMPLETE THE STRESS CYCLE

When you flip into a stressed state (fight-flight-freeze-fawn), you need to complete the stress cycle to release that energy. The problem in modern society is that many of us get stuck in the stress cycle. After learning about the stress cycle in Chapter 4, come back to this page and write down the ways you complete the cycle. Do you use movement, laughter, breath work, or other techniques?

MAP YOUR NERVOUS SYSTEM

Nervous system mapping is tracking where you are in your nervous system, to give you information about what you need in any given moment. You can read more about this in Chapter 4. Where in your nervous system you spend the most time—hyperarousal; window of tolerance; or a shut-down, hypoarousal state? And what helps you get back into your window of tolerance?

STRENGTHEN NERVOUS SYSTEM RESILIENCE

Adopting practices like consistent physical activity, staying hydrated, eating nutrient-rich foods, addressing unhelpful thought habits, and practicing stress management techniques can significantly bolster nervous system resilience. Which of these techniques do you already practice? Write them down here.

RESET YOUR NERVOUS SYSTEM

Integrating nervous system resets into your daily routine, such as taking three deep breaths every time you check your email, can be helpful for maintaining balance and reducing stress. Jot down when you could use a nervous system reset.

Consider Psychological and Mindset Work

Expanding your bucket's capacity largely involves what I call "deep work." This concept encompasses the significant psychological effort required to embrace your neurodivergent identity and the intensive process of learning to interact with the world (and yourself) in new ways.

Key aspects of this deep psychological work include confronting and reducing people-pleasing behaviors, embracing your neurodivergent identity, transforming unhelpful relational dynamics, and challenging internalized ableism. Engaging in these practices not only broadens your capacity but also strengthens your resilience.

Integrating Your Neurodivergent Identity

If you are recovering from chronic or late-in-life Autistic burnout, you may need more than rest and added accommodations. You may find yourself restructuring your sense of self as you incorporate your neurodivergent identity.

Many people don't discover their autism until they are already in burnout. And so your burnout may be the first time you recognize that your life simply isn't working. You may discover you are working yourself into the ground trying to function in an allistic world, and it's not sustainable.

If this is your experience, your recovery will likely also include:

1 Acknowledging internalized ableism

2 Creating space for grief

Acknowledging Internalized Ableism

"Internalized ableism" refers to beliefs and prejudices you hold, whether consciously or not, that come from living in an ableist society. These beliefs often form your expectations about yourself. For example, "I should be able to work a forty-hour work week" or "I shouldn't need accommodations."

Internalized ableism drives many of your unrealistic expectations of yourself. You are holding yourself to an allistic "normal" while not honoring your unique sensory, communication, and bodily needs. You will continue to run yourself ragged until you address this internalized ableism (and these expectations)!

Grief Work

Grief work goes hand in hand with addressing internalized ableism. As you address your ableism, you also encounter your limits. It's okay to grieve your limits. In order to accept new ones, you need to grieve "what is."

To accept your limits, you have to grieve the idea of yourself that you are releasing. After my autism discovery, I realized my physical limits would never magically disappear. I realized I would always live in a body that needed more rest and was limited by its sensory needs. I grieved what this meant for me. The careers I would no longer be pursuing, and the ways this limited my social world and my role as a parent. I needed to grieve the image I had of myself to embrace who I was.

Unlearning People-Pleasing

Another area where Autistic people often need to focus is to try to stop people-pleasing. Masking gets baked into our psyches and is deeper than simply mimicking scripts and body postures. This can result in our becoming perpetual people-pleasers. Masking and people-pleasing make it hard to maintain healthy boundaries.

Unlearning this through addressing internalized ableism and learning to be in relationships with others while maintaining healthy boundaries is a key part of recovery. If you perpetually define your identity based on how pleased others are with you, you will remain stuck in the frantic loop of overperforming and burnout. There are many ways to engage in this depth work: reading, journaling, writing, connecting with other Autistic people, processing with trusted others, or working with a therapist or coach.

★ ★ ★
EXAMPLE

At-a-Glance Ways to Expand Your Bucket

MANAGE YOUR ENERGY	FOCUS ON BELONGING AND SUPPORT	ADJUST YOUR LIFESTYLE
▶ Implement a pacing system to manage energy levels ▶ Dedicate time to my special interests to spark energy	▶ Join an online Autistic community for support and connection ▶ Listen to Autistic-focused podcasts to immerse in Autistic culture	▶ Aim for twenty minutes of walking daily for physical health
PRIORITIZE AND IMPROVE YOUR SLEEP	**PRACTICE SELF-ADVOCACY**	**LEAN INTO YOUR AUTISTIC STRENGTHS**
▶ Modify my sleep environment to improve sleep hygiene ▶ Establish a five-minute sleep routine	▶ Inquire about workplace accommodations ▶ Ask my partner for additional support this week	▶ Explore additional ways to integrate my special interests into daily life ▶ Identify and engage in activities that align with my personal values
LOOK FOR SELF-INSIGHT	**REGULATE YOUR NERVOUS SYSTEM**	**CONSIDER PSYCHOLOGICAL AND MINDSET WORK**
▶ Use an alexithymia app for five minutes a day to improve emotional identification ▶ Use a mood tracker	▶ Incorporate three cleansing breaths every time I open email ▶ Practice nervous system mapping	▶ Work on addressing internalized ableism ▶ Go to therapy ▶ Develop and practice setting healthy boundaries

At-a-Glance Ways to Expand Your Bucket

MANAGE YOUR ENERGY	FOCUS ON BELONGING AND SUPPORT	ADJUST YOUR LIFESTYLE

PRIORITIZE AND IMPROVE YOUR SLEEP	PRACTICE SELF-ADVOCACY	LEAN INTO YOUR AUTISTIC STRENGTHS

LOOK FOR SELF-INSIGHT	REGULATE YOUR NERVOUS SYSTEM	CONSIDER PSYCHOLOGICAL AND MINDSET WORK

CREATE YOUR OWN!

CHAPTER 3

Regulating Your Sensory Experience

Cultivating a Sensory Lens to Better Understand Burnout

Your senses, which are integral to your nervous system, shape your interaction with the environment around you. At the heart of Autistic burnout is, essentially, nervous system burnout. This explains the heightened sensory sensitivities many of us face during times of burnout. It's like our nervous system is operating in overdrive! Additionally, chronic sensory overload can trigger or worsen burnout.

Therefore, grasping the nuances of your sensory system and adopting sensory strategies are key in both mitigating the effects of burnout and preventing its onset. The journey to greater agency over your sensory system begins with what I refer to as developing a "sensory lens."

Cultivating a sensory lens helps you shift from a reactive stance to a proactive one and tune into your sensory experiences more thoughtfully. Having a sensory lens involves:

IDENTIFYING YOUR SENSORY LIKES:
Determining what things bring you comfort and joy.

UNDERSTANDING YOUR SENSORY TRIGGERS:
Recognizing sensory irritants and their effects on your nervous system, emotions, thoughts, and behaviors.

FINDING YOUR SENSORY SOOTHERS AND HELPERS:
Sensory soothers are things that help calm and regulate you during times of high stress. Helpers are specific accommodations and tools, such as tinted glasses or fidget spinners, that can support you during demanding sensory experiences.

In addition, determining your sensory profile—in other words, whether you are a sensory seeker or avoider—is another way to more deeply understand your sensory experience. Overall, though, simply being mindful of the sensory situations embedded in daily activities can enable you to tailor your surroundings. You can use your newly cultivated sensory lens to identify and fully understand the implications of the sensory experiences around you.

Much of the foundation for my work in sensory profiles is inspired by occupational therapist Dr. Tina Champagne. Some of her work can be found here: Tina Champagne, "Sensory Approaches," in *Developing Positive Cultures of Care: Resource Guide*, 3rd ed., eds. J. LeBel and N. Stromberg (Boston: Massachusetts Department of Mental Health, 2012), https://mass.gov/doc/sensory-approaches/download.

My Own Experience Cultivating a Sensory Lens

At thirty-seven, after my autism discovery, I began to question and examine the lifelong dance I'd been doing to avoid certain sensory experiences. I had learned to navigate my world with quiet adaptations, like waking up early to get to the grocery store the moment it opened, and steering clear of all scented products and people adorned with perfume or cologne. Despite these adjustments, it never occurred to me that I might have sensory issues. It was a revelation to find that not everyone experienced the world with as much intensity as I did.

> While the concept of a sensory lens might appear simple, many Autistic people find themselves disconnected from their bodies or struggling with body awareness, due to interoception differences, masking, or trauma.

This disconnection can obscure our sensory experiences, sometimes to the point where we only recognize irritation or overwhelm in moments of intense distress. For example, I recognized my aversions to certain stimuli (like specific laundry detergents, perfumes, or striped shirts) but didn't connect these dislikes with broader sensory sensitivities until I began intentionally focusing on cultivating a sensory lens.

> Cultivating a sensory lens means attentively observing how various sensations affect you—emotionally, mentally, and physically.

It's about recognizing the impact of specific sounds, textures, smells, tastes, and visual stimuli on your mood, energy levels, and general well-being.

The next several pages outline practices for building sensory awareness. Among these, my personal go-to method is using sensory checklists. These checklists are designed to assist in identifying and recording your sensory likes, triggers, and soothers, thereby deepening your understanding of your sensory preferences and needs.

Effective Ways to Cultivate a Sensory Lens

When working to cultivate a sensory lens, here are some practices that can be helpful. Check any that you think might work for you.

Mindful check-ins:
Mindfulness practices (like body scans or brief mindful check-ins) enhance body and sensory awareness.

Sensory checklists:
Sensory checklists are a great way to record what you like (and don't like!). Quickly identify likes, dislikes, and what energizes you.

Sensory journal:
Create a sensory journal to track triggers, likes, and responses to sensory inputs. This process will help you identify patterns over time.

Sensory play:
Play is a great way to get to know your sensory system! Learn what kinds of textures, sounds, movement, and weight feel good.

Sensory check-ins:
Feeling off, anxious, or tired? But aren't sure why? Do a quick sensory scan of your environment to see if there is a sensory irritant or cause.

Discover whether you're a sensory seeker or avoider:
Gain a deeper understanding of your sensory profile by reflecting on whether you are a sensory seeker or a sensory avoider. Where do you have dulled senses? And where are your senses heightened?

Do You Seek or Avoid Sensory Experiences?

This chapter will guide you in mapping out your sensory experiences, which will in turn help you develop a sensory lens. Specifically, we'll be looking at your sensory preferences, triggers, and soothers. As you map out your sensory experiences it is also helpful to pay attention to where you are a sensory seeker and where you are sensory avoidant. It's not unusual for Autistic people to display both seeking and avoidant behaviors. This can vary between different senses, but also may change over time.

For instance, I find visual clutter, stripes, and bright lights overwhelming, making me **sensory avoidant** visually. However, when it comes to taste, I'm drawn to spicy, salty, and crunchy foods, **seeking out** intense flavors as a form of self-soothing. Mapping out your preferences will help you recognize where you seek out sensory experiences and where you avoid them, which can give you insight into how to use sensory input to soothe you, energize you, or help you focus.

If you want a deeper dive, a professional such as an occupational therapist or sensory-aware therapist can help you map your sensory experiences (clinically referred to as your sensory profile). While this book doesn't guide you through creating a full sensory profile, the exercises in this chapter will help you identify patterns in your likes, triggers, and soothers, revealing your tendencies toward sensory seeking or avoidance.

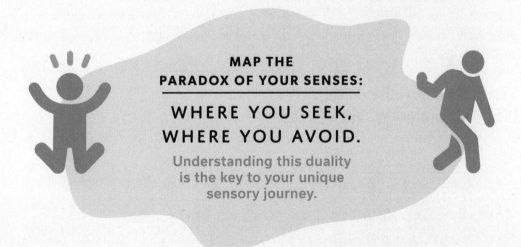

**MAP THE
PARADOX OF YOUR SENSES:**

WHERE YOU SEEK, WHERE YOU AVOID.

Understanding this duality
is the key to your unique
sensory journey.

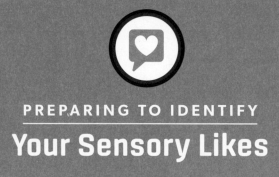

Your Sensory Likes

Cultivating your sensory lens involves mapping out your sensory preferences and aversions. This step, while seemingly straightforward, is pivotal. The distance you may have placed between you and your true sensory experiences—whether through disconnecting from your body or masking—muddies the waters of your sensory understanding. So, don't be deceived by this seemingly simple first task of identifying your likes! It's possible this skill (knowing what you like) is one that needs cultivating too. Here are some other things to keep in mind.

Be Patient and Gentle with Yourself

Increasing sensory awareness can be challenging or uncomfortable for some. This exploration might stir feelings of unease as you confront long-ignored or masked sensations. If you have disconnected from your body, you did so for a good reason! So, deepening that connection can feel alarming. If you find yourself in this position, consider working one-on-one with a therapist while you go through this process and take a gradual approach.

Exploring Your Authentic Self

Exploring your sensory preferences and needs is actually a form of self-advocacy and a move toward getting to know your authentic self. It allows you to honor your true experiences and build a bridge to your inner self while nurturing your sensory well-being in a way that guards against burnout.

Checklists Can Help You Organize Your Preferences

For those who find tuning into body awareness a challenge, sensory checklists serve as a practical entry point. These tools are not meant to be exhaustive but rather a beginning, a way to spark your curiosity and guide you toward the sensory inputs that bring you comfort, joy, and delight!

Identify Your Sensory Likes

Check any items that resonate with you, and add your own ideas in the blank spaces provided.

LIGHTING

- Natural lighting
- Dim lighting
- Bright lighting
- Artificial light
- Colorful lighting (LED)
- Moderate lighting
- Yellow hues (warm lighting)
- White hues (cool spectrum)

OTHER:
- _____
- _____
- _____
- _____

SMELL

- Mild or subtle scents
- Fresh or clean smells
- Citrusy or fruity scents
- Food-related scents
- Herbal or earthy scents
- Aromatherapy scents (e.g., lavender, eucalyptus)
- Natural scents (e.g., flowers, trees)
- Specific scents that bring joyful memories

OTHER:
- _____
- _____
- _____
- _____

SOUND

- Quiet
- White noise
- Brown noise
- Binaural beats
- Loud and lively
- Music/background noise
- Television on in background
- Stim song (song on repeat)

OTHER:
- _____
- _____
- _____

VISUAL

- Visually sparse and organized
- Neutral colors
- Vibrant colors
- Patterns and bright decor
- Solid colors
- Minimalism
- Everything spread out/ visible

OTHER:
- _____
- _____
- _____
- _____

TACTILE

- Light touch
- Deep pressure touch
- No touch
- Twirling hair
- Fidget toys
- Soft textures
- Petting a dog or cat
- Warm bath or shower

OTHER:
- _____
- _____
- _____
- _____

TASTE/TEXTURE

- Chewing gum
- Crunchy snacks
- Chewing ice
- Spicy food
- Drinking a warm beverage
- Hard candy
- Drinking a carbonated drink

OTHER:
- _____
- _____
- _____

CONTINUED ▶

CLOTHING

- Constrictive or compression clothing (tight)
- Loose-fitting clothing
- Cotton fabric
- Tagless clothing
- Seamless garments
- Breathable materials
- Soft and gentle textures
- Stretchy, flexible clothing
- Moisture-wicking fabrics
- Nonirritating fabrics (e.g., organic cotton, modal)
- Adjustable closures (e.g., Velcro, snaps)
- Weighted vest
- Nonrestrictive waistbands (e.g., elastic-free)
- Layering options for temperature regulation
- Odor-resistant or hypoallergenic materials
- Beanies or hats that provide pressure

OTHER:
- _____
- _____
- _____
- _____
- _____
- _____
- _____
- _____
- _____

MOVEMENT

- Gentle rocking or swaying
- Swinging
- Jumping or bouncing
- Stimming
- Spinning or twirling
- Pacing or walking
- Repetitive movements (e.g., hand flapping, tapping)
- Weighted or deep-pressure activities
- Proprioceptive activities (e.g., pushing against objects, lifting weights)

OTHER:
- _____
- _____
- _____
- _____
- _____

ENVIRONMENT

- Outdoors
- Indoors
- Open space
- Nooks and crannies
- Urban environments
- Rural settings

OTHER:
- _____
- _____
- _____
- _____
- _____
- _____
- _____

TEMPERATURE

- Cool
- Warm
- Breeze/airflow
- Neutral temperature

OTHER:
- _____
- _____
- _____
- _____

PROPRIOCEPTION

- Lifting weights
- Pressure
- Weight
- No pressure (avoidance)
- Pillow/weighted blanket
- Weight on lap

OTHER:
- _____
- _____
- _____
- _____

PEOPLE

- Lots of people
- Only a few people
- A small group of people
- No people
- People you don't know

OTHER:
- _____
- _____
- _____
- _____
- _____

Your Sensory Likes at a Glance

Now that you have completed the sensory preference checklist, it can be helpful to compile your preferences on one page so you can quickly and easily refer to and review them. Consider taking a picture to have a digital version easily stored on your phone.

LIGHTING	VISUAL	SMELL

TACTILE	SOUND	TASTE/TEXTURE

CLOTHING	MOVEMENT	ENVIRONMENT

TEMPERATURE	PROPRIOCEPTION	PEOPLE

Reflect on Your Sensory Likes and Profile

As you worked through the checklist, did you notice any recurring patterns or gain new insights into your sensory experiences? Take a moment to reflect on any new discoveries you learned about your sensory preferences.

Now list any areas where you've identified a pattern of **sensory avoidance** in your sensory likes:

▶ _____

▶ _____

▶ _____

▶ _____

▶ _____

▶ _____

▶ _____

List any areas where you've identified a pattern of **sensory seeking** in your sensory likes:

▶ _____

▶ _____

▶ _____

▶ _____

▶ _____

▶ _____

▶ _____

Your Sensory Triggers

It's important to uncover and understand the sensory triggers that impact you. These triggers, whether visual, auditory, olfactory, gustatory, or tactile, can be elusive, especially for those of us navigating challenges with interoception (body awareness) or those accustomed to coping through detachment. It's often only in the *aftermath* of a headache or meltdown that the influence of these triggers becomes clear.

If you struggle with interoception, here are some strategies to help you identify triggers:

- ▶ **WRITE IN A SENSORY JOURNAL:** Consider keeping a simple journal (or use a notes app) to track your environment and responses. Over time, this can help you spot patterns.

- ▶ **SET CHECK-IN ALARMS:** Set gentle reminders on your phone to pause and check in with how you're doing. These regular check-ins can help you catch unnoticed triggers.

- ▶ **ASK FOR FEEDBACK:** Ask trusted people if they notice you behaving differently in certain environments.

- ▶ **TRACK PHYSICAL SYMPTOMS AND BEHAVIOR CHANGES:** If tracking feelings is tough, try noting changes in your behavior or physical symptoms like headaches. Over time, see if you can connect these to specific environments or sensory experiences.

Once you've identified these triggers, you gain the ability to be more proactive in preparing for them and developing strategies that allow you to **anticipate and reduce sensory challenges before they escalate**. This method empowers you to better advocate for your needs and **live more harmoniously within your sensory environments**, transforming your approach from one of mere reaction to one of thoughtful anticipation and planning.

Uncover Your Sensory Triggers

Check any items that resonate with you, and add your
own ideas in the blank spaces provided.

LIGHTING

- ○ Bright or harsh lighting
- ○ Flickering or flashing lights
- ○ Fluorescent lighting
- ○ Intense or direct sunlight
- ○ Rapid changes in lighting
- ○ Dim or low lighting
- ○ Glare or reflections
- ○ Colored or neon lights
- ○ Strobe lights
- ○ Rapidly moving or flashing visuals

OTHER:
- ○ _____
- ○ _____

SMELL

- ○ Strong odors
- ○ Chemical smells
- ○ Perfumes or colognes
- ○ Cooking smells
- ○ Certain foods
- ○ Smoke or pollution
- ○ Cleaning products
- ○ Floral or fragrant scents

OTHER:
- ○ _____
- ○ _____
- ○ _____
- ○ _____
- ○ _____

SOUND

- ○ Loud noises
- ○ Sudden bursts of sound
- ○ Background noise or chatter
- ○ Echoes or reverberations
- ○ Busy environments
- ○ People chewing
- ○ Certain types of music or specific instruments
- ○ High-pitched or piercing sounds
- ○ Repetitive or constant noise (e.g., pen clicking)

OTHER:
- ○ _____

VISUAL

- ○ Busy visual environments
- ○ Cluttered environments
- ○ Specific colors or contrasts
- ○ Overwhelming patterns or designs
- ○ Certain types of visual media (e.g., fast-paced movies or video games)
- ○ Strained or intense eye contact

OTHER:
- ○ _____
- ○ _____

TACTILE

- ○ Rough or abrasive textures
- ○ Itchy or scratchy materials
- ○ Light or gentle touch
- ○ Heavy or deep pressure
- ○ Wet or sticky sensations
- ○ Moisture
- ○ Sensitivity to temperature (e.g., hot or cold objects)

OTHER:
- ○ _____
- ○ _____
- ○ _____

TASTE/TEXTURE

- ○ Overpowering flavors
- ○ Spicy or hot foods
- ○ Bitter tastes
- ○ Sour tastes
- ○ Sweet tastes
- ○ Food touching sensitivities
- ○ Food temperature issues
- ○ Unfamiliar or new foods
- ○ Textural experiences (e.g., mushy)
- ○ Sensitivities or allergies to certain ingredients

OTHER:
- ○ _____

CLOTHING

- Rough or scratchy fabrics
- Tags or labels on clothing
- Tight or constrictive clothing
- Loose or baggy clothing
- Clothing that is too tight around specific body parts
- Uncomfortable or restrictive footwear
- Specific textures, patterns, or colors that bother you
- Sensitivity to certain types of fabric (e.g., wool, lace)

OTHER:
- _____
- _____
- _____
- _____
- _____
- _____

MOVEMENT

- Erratic movements
- Intense or excessive physical activity
- Certain types of transport (elevators, escalators, etc.)

OTHER:
- _____
- _____
- _____
- _____
- _____

ENVIRONMENT

- Crowded or busy spaces
- Confined environments
- Overly cluttered or disorganized environments
- Lack of personal space or privacy
- Unfamiliar environments
- High-traffic areas with limited escape routes
- Unpredictable or rapidly changing environments

OTHER:
- _____
- _____
- _____
- _____
- _____
- _____

TEMPERATURE

- Extreme heat
- Extreme cold
- Stuffy or stagnant air
- Drafts or breezes
- Humidity or dryness
- Overheating or being too bundled up
- Intense temperature variations

OTHER:
- _____
- _____
- _____
- _____
- _____

PEOPLE

- Loud or intrusive voices
- Prolonged eye contact
- Personal space invasion
- Social demands and small talk
- Physical touch or proximity to others
- Unpredictable or unexpected movements from others
- Overstimulating social interactions or group settings
- Specific facial expressions or gestures

OTHER:
- _____
- _____
- _____
- _____
- _____
- _____
- _____
- _____
- _____
- _____

Your Sensory Triggers at a Glance

Now that you've completed the sensory trigger checklist, it may be helpful to compile your preferences on one page for quick and easy reference. You might consider taking a picture to keep a digital version on your phone. Sharing this with close friends or family members can also help them better understand you and your needs.

LIGHTING	VISUAL	SMELL

TACTILE	SOUND	TASTE/TEXTURE

CLOTHING	MOVEMENT	ENVIRONMENT

TEMPERATURE	PEOPLE	OTHER

Reflect on Your Sensory Triggers and Profile

As you went through the checklist, did you observe any recurring patterns or gain fresh insights into your sensory experiences? Take a moment now to map out any new discoveries you learned about your sensory triggers and sensory aversions.

Now list any areas where you've identified a pattern of **sensory avoidance** in your triggers:

▶ _____

▶ _____

▶ _____

▶ _____

▶ _____

▶ _____

▶ _____

List any areas where you've identified a pattern of **sensory seeking** in your triggers (for example, if you have a strong aversion to silence or minimalism, this may indicate sensory seeking tendencies):

▶ _____

▶ _____

▶ _____

▶ _____

▶ _____

▶ _____

▶ _____

PREPARING TO DISCOVER

Your Sensory Soothers and Helpers

The last step of exploring your sensory experiences is to identify the things that help calm and regulate you during times of distress or discomfort. These are your sensory soothers.

You may notice some overlap with your sensory preferences; however, sensory soothing activities and items are different because **they are specifically designed to restore sensory regulation** when you are experiencing sensory overload.

Sensory helpers are the tools and resources that assist you in navigating your sensory environment, whether by **blocking overwhelming input or providing pleasant sensory input**.

By exploring sensory soothers and incorporating them into your daily routine, you can create a personalized tool kit or **create sensory detox rituals** to help you regain regulation in the face of sensory challenges.

Discover Your Sensory Soothers

LIGHTING

- Darkness
- Soft or dim lighting
- Natural light or daylight
- Himalayan salt lamp
- Candlelight
- Soothing ambient lighting
- Twinkle or fairy lights
- Light-filtering glasses
- Light projector with calming images

OTHER:
- _____
- _____
- _____

VISUAL

- Nature scenery
- Calming artwork
- Closing eyes/visual detox
- Photographs
- Soft, muted color palettes
- View of water or nature
- Lava lamp or bubble lamp
- Guided imagery
- Visual-stimulation apps or programs
- Engaging in coloring, watercolor painting, or paint by numbers

OTHER:
- _____
- _____

SMELL

- Essential oils or sachets
- Freshly brewed coffee or tea
- Baking or food aromas
- Scented candles
- Fresh flowers or plants
- Vanilla, chamomile, lavender, or other calming scents
- Scented stress balls or sensory toys for on-the-go scent stimulation

OTHER:
- _____
- _____
- _____

SOUND

- Noise-canceling headphones, loops, or ear defenders
- A stim song playlist
- Calming music
- Instrumental tunes
- Nature sounds
- White or green noise (machine or app)
- ASMR videos
- Guided meditation
- Soft, soothing voices

OTHER:
- _____
- _____
- _____

TACTILE

- Taking a warm bath or shower with different textures (e.g., washcloths, loofahs)
- Engaging in tactile crafts or hobbies, such as pottery, sculpting, or knitting
- Exploring sensory bins or tactile sensory play with materials like rice, sand, or water beads
- Enjoying the sensation of running fingers through Kinetic Sand or Play-Doh
- Engaging in activities like gardening or working with soil, or earthing (walking barefoot in nature)
- Using fidget toys or stress balls to engage the hands and relieve tension
- Seeking out opportunities for touch-based activities, such as receiving a massage or practicing partner yoga
- Using a weighted blanket or stuffie, or weighted garments

OTHER:
- _____
- _____
- _____
- _____
- _____

CONTINUED ▶

TASTE/TEXTURE

- Savoring a favorite comfort food, safe food, or treat
- Enjoying a warm cup of tea or hot chocolate
- Exploring different flavors and textures through mindful eating
- Trying soothing foods like smoothies or soups
- Experimenting with comforting flavors like vanilla, cinnamon, or honey
- Sampling different types of chocolate or other indulgent desserts
- Exploring herbal teas or infusions known for their calming properties

OTHER:
- _____
- _____
- _____
- _____
- _____

CLOTHING

- Soft, gentle textures
- Tagless clothing
- Loose-fitting clothing
- Stretchy clothing

OTHER:
- _____
- _____
- _____
- _____
- _____

MOVEMENT

- Gentle stretching or yoga
- Rocking or swaying
- Walking or hiking in nature
- Swinging or swaying motion
- Dancing
- Slow and rhythmic movement
- Jumping on a trampoline or bouncing on an exercise ball
- Exercise balls or balance boards for proprioceptive input

OTHER:
- _____
- _____
- _____

ENVIRONMENT

- Decluttered surroundings
- Cozy and comfortable seating
- Soft and soothing colors in the surroundings
- Organizing workplace to be visually pleasing
- Access to a quiet and secluded area
- Incorporation of natural elements (e.g., plants, natural light)

OTHER:
- _____
- _____
- _____
- _____
- _____

TEMPERATURE

- Warm or cozy blankets
- Cooling gel packs or ice packs
- Warm or cool compress
- Heating pad
- Hot or cold beverage
- Warm shower or bath
- Air conditioner or fan

OTHER:
- _____
- _____
- _____
- _____
- _____
- _____
- _____

PEOPLE

- Time alone
- A designated advocate
- A supportive friend
- Opportunities for meaningful connections
- Using communication strategies or visual supports to express needs
- Access to support groups or online communities

OTHER:
- _____
- _____
- _____
- _____

Record Your Sensory Helpers

While sensory soothers often involve actions you can take, think of sensory helpers as the sensory aids or supports you lean on when stressed. Check any items that resonate with you, and add your own ideas in the blank spaces provided.

VISUAL

- Tinted glasses or sunglasses for light sensitivity
- Eye masks or sleep masks for visual relaxation
- Colored overlays for reading or reducing visual stress
- Cold eye mask
- Lava lamp for visual stimulation

OTHER:
- _____
- _____
- _____
- _____
- _____
- _____

SMELL

- Scented candles or wax melts
- Aromatic sachets or pouches
- Essential oil diffuser with calming scents
- Aromatherapy
- Scented stress balls or sensory toys for on-the-go scent stimulation
- Scented drawer liners or scented drawer sachets for pleasant scents in storage

OTHER:
- _____
- _____
- _____
- _____
- _____
- _____

TACTILE AND CLOTHING SUPPORTS

- Soft and plush textures (e.g., plushies, blankets)
- Sensory balls or fidget toys with different textures
- Weighted blanket or lap pad
- Fidget spinners or textured fidget rings or bracelets
- Squishy stress balls or sensory gel pads
- Compression clothing (e.g., weighted vests, tight-fitting garments)
- Squeeze toys or stress-relief objects like Kinetic Sand
- Textured surfaces for tactile exploration (e.g., textured mats, fabrics)

- Therapy brushes or vibrating massagers for sensory modulation
- TENS Unit (a small device that delivers mild electrical impulses to reduce pain by stimulating nerves, but can also provide sensory support)
- Weighted heating pad

OTHER:
- _____
- _____
- _____
- _____
- _____

SOUND

- Noise-canceling headphones, loops, or ear defenders
- White noise machines
- A stim song playlist

OTHER:
- _____
- _____
- _____
- _____
- _____
- _____
- _____
- _____

CONTINUED ▶

TASTE/TEXTURE	MOVEMENT	TEMPERATURE
● Chewable jewelry	● Sensory tools for hand manipulation	● Hot or cold beverage
● Chewing gum	● Swings or hammocks for gentle rocking	● Warm or cozy blankets
● Crunchy snacks	● Exercise balls or balance boards for proprioceptive input	● Heating pad
● Toothpicks		● Warm or cool compress
● Oral sensory tools (e.g., chewy tubes, chewable pencil tops)		● Cooling gel packs or ice packs
		● Air conditioner or fan for airflow

OTHER:

TASTE/TEXTURE
● _____
● _____
● _____
● _____
● _____
● _____
● _____
● _____
● _____
● _____

MOVEMENT
OTHER:
● _____
● _____
● _____
● _____
● _____
● _____
● _____
● _____
● _____
● _____

TEMPERATURE
OTHER:
● _____
● _____
● _____
● _____
● _____
● _____
● _____
● _____
● _____
● _____

Your Sensory Soothers and Helpers at a Glance

Now that you have completed the sensory soothers and helpers checklists, it can be helpful to compile your preferences on one page for quick and easy reference. You might consider taking a picture to keep a digital version on your phone. Sharing this with close friends or family members can also help them better understand you and your needs.

LIGHTING	VISUAL	SMELL

TACTILE	SOUND	TASTE/TEXTURE

CLOTHING	MOVEMENT	ENVIRONMENT

TEMPERATURE	PEOPLE	OTHER

Reflect on Your Sensory Soothers and Helpers

As you went through the checklists, did you observe any recurring patterns or gain fresh insights into your sensory experiences? Take a moment now to reflect on any new discoveries you had about your sensory soothers and helpers.

Now list any areas where you've identified a pattern of **sensory avoidance** in your sensory soothers or helpers (for example, if most of your helpers were things that help block out sensory input, that would be an indication you tend to be more sensory avoidant).

▶ _____

▶ _____

▶ _____

▶ _____

▶ _____

▶ _____

▶ _____

List areas where you've identified a pattern of **sensory seeking** in your sensory soothers or helpers (for example, if most of your sensory supports involved adding sensory inputs like smells, crunchy foods, or music, this may indicate that taking in sensory input soothes you).

▶ _____

▶ _____

▶ _____

▶ _____

▶ _____

▶ _____

▶ _____

Map Out Your Sensory System

Now that you've completed the sensory checklists and reflected on how you engage in sensory seeking and avoidance behaviors, let's bring it all together by mapping out your sensory system. The first row on this page shows an example of how to fill out this template—then you can fill in your own responses. List the specific ways you seek out sensory input in the "Seeking Behavior" boxes and note how you avoid or block out sensory input in the "Avoidance Behavior" boxes. Finally, in the summary box, circle the term that best describes your overall experience: "Seeker," "Avoider," or "Mixed," and add any relevant notes.

VISUAL SEEKING BEHAVIOR	VISUAL AVOIDANCE BEHAVIOR	SUMMARY
I enjoy looking at water, waves, and bubbles.	*I avoid bright light (always wearing sunglasses).* *Patterns and visual contrast trigger headaches.* *Busy movement irritates me.* *Visual clutter stresses me out.*	Seeker (Avoider) Mixed **NOTES:** *Mostly avoidant, but find patterned and predictable movement soothing.*

EXAMPLE

VISUAL SEEKING BEHAVIOR	VISUAL AVOIDANCE BEHAVIOR	SUMMARY
		Seeker Avoider Mixed **NOTES:**

CONTINUED ▶

SMELL SEEKING BEHAVIOR	SMELL AVOIDANCE BEHAVIOR	SUMMARY
		Seeker
		Avoider
		Mixed
		NOTES:

TACTILE SEEKING BEHAVIOR	TACTILE AVOIDANCE BEHAVIOR	SUMMARY
		Seeker
		Avoider
		Mixed
		NOTES:

SOUND SEEKING BEHAVIOR	SOUND AVOIDANCE BEHAVIOR	SUMMARY
		Seeker
		Avoider
		Mixed
		NOTES:

TASTE/TEXTURE SEEKING BEHAVIOR	TASTE/TEXTURE AVOIDANCE BEHAVIOR	SUMMARY
		Seeker Avoider Mixed NOTES:

MOVEMENT SEEKING BEHAVIOR	MOVEMENT AVOIDANCE BEHAVIOR	SUMMARY
		Seeker Avoider Mixed NOTES:

PROPRIOCEPTION SEEKING BEHAVIOR	PROPRIOCEPTION AVOIDANCE BEHAVIOR	SUMMARY
		Seeker Avoider Mixed NOTES:

How to Build a Sensory Soothing Kit

Now that you have identified your sensory likes, triggers, and soothers/helpers, you can put all this insight and knowledge into action by building a sensory soothing kit! This is a physical kit that you can take with you on the run so you're always prepared. Follow these steps to make your kit.

STEP ONE

Select a Container

First, grab a container to hold your items. This can be whatever you'd like, from a small, discreet pouch to something larger like a lunch box or tote bag. As long as it's portable, can fit your items, and will keep them organized and accessible, it'll work!

If you have the space for it, you could also dedicate an area of your home to become a sensory spot where all your sensory soothing kit items are stored so they're always available when you need them. This can greatly reduce the stress of trying to find them when you're already feeling overwhelmed.

STEP TWO

Consider Your Needs

After you have your container, go back and review your likes, triggers, and soothers/helpers and think about what sensory inputs help you feel calm and grounded.

Select Sensory Tools

Now that you know what sensory inputs help you to regulate, it's time to pick out your sensory tools. Based on your preferences, gather various tools that can help soothe and regulate your senses. Here are some ideas of what you might include in your kit:

Visual Tools

- Water fidget toys like a liquid motion bubbler or mini water game
- Fidget spinners
- Glitter jars
- Tinted sunglasses
- Bubbles

Smell Tools

- Essential oils
- Scented lotions
- Aromatic sachets
- Scented lip balm

Sound Tools

- Noise-canceling headphones
- Earplugs
- Soothing music or audio recordings

Tactile Tools

- Fidget toys
- Textured objects (e.g., squishy balls, textured fabrics)
- Stress balls
- Weighted lap pads

Taste/ Texture Tools

- Gum or mints
- Crunchy or chewy snacks
- Lollipops
- Toothpicks

Prioritize Your Sensory Regulation

Understanding and addressing your sensory needs is a powerful step in managing Autistic burnout. When your sensory system is dysregulated, it is significantly more challenging to manage your behaviors, thoughts, and emotions. In other words, **when your foundational sensory system is off-kilter, everything else tends to follow suit**! That's why making sensory wellness a priority is key for creating a life that's resilient to Autistic burnout.

Self-attunement forms the cornerstone of sensory self-care. If you are able to tune into your needs moment by moment, you will begin to **learn what you need and when**. My hope is that through completing the checklists and practicing the strategies discussed in this chapter you will become more attuned to yourself. The sensory lens you're cultivating can help you **more effectively manage your sensory experiences** on a day-to-day basis. And since your sensory system is part of your nervous system, you'll be nurturing your nervous system as well. We'll discuss your nervous system next.

 When your foundational sensory system is off-kilter, everything else tends to follow suit! That's why *making sensory wellness a priority is key* for creating a life that's resilient to Autistic burnout.

CHAPTER 4

Managing Your Nervous System

Understanding the Neurodivergent Nervous System

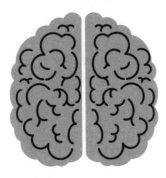

Autism is widely recognized as a distinct neurotype, but have you considered it in terms of a unique nervous system? **Autistic individuals possess a neurology that is highly sensitive**, taking in the world with acute depth and heightened perception. Furthermore, we have what I call a more "rigid nervous system"—in other words, one that struggles to take in and adapt to incoming stressors. This means that we experience the world with heightened sensitivity and more difficulty processing several sources of sensory input at once.

This heightened sensitivity sheds an important light on Autistic burnout. In fact, **burnout can be seen as a form of chronic nervous system dysregulation**. This overload often results from stressors that are not effectively managed or mitigated. Viewing burnout through this lens offers some insight into why we are so vulnerable to it. In addition to the increased vulnerability and reduced flexibility of the Autistic nervous system, we also encounter a high number of stressors—from trauma and social victimization to sensory upheaval. It's no wonder burnout is a prevalent issue! Thus, **understanding your nervous system and working in alignment with it is a key part of preventing and recovering from burnout**.

In this chapter, we'll dive into the complexities of the Autistic nervous system, offering a primer on nervous system basics. We'll explore the concept of the "window of tolerance"—the optimal zone for managing stress—and how to map your nervous system's responses. Finally, we'll discuss strategies for training your nervous system to complete the stress cycle.

Nervous System?

What do we mean by the "nervous system," especially in terms of emotional regulation and stress response? Let's take a step back and view the nervous system as a vast, complex network. It's divided into two main branches, each playing distinct roles while also collaborating to keep you functional and responsive to your surroundings:

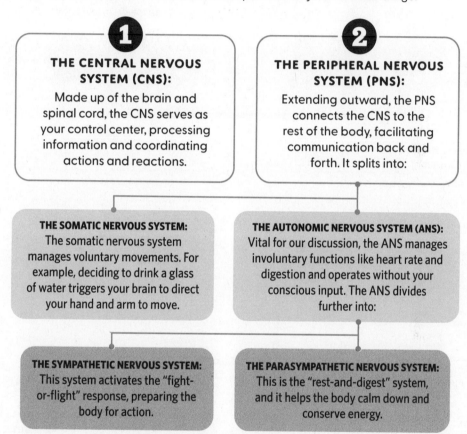

1

THE CENTRAL NERVOUS SYSTEM (CNS):
Made up of the brain and spinal cord, the CNS serves as your control center, processing information and coordinating actions and reactions.

2

THE PERIPHERAL NERVOUS SYSTEM (PNS):
Extending outward, the PNS connects the CNS to the rest of the body, facilitating communication back and forth. It splits into:

THE SOMATIC NERVOUS SYSTEM:
The somatic nervous system manages voluntary movements. For example, deciding to drink a glass of water triggers your brain to direct your hand and arm to move.

THE AUTONOMIC NERVOUS SYSTEM (ANS):
Vital for our discussion, the ANS manages involuntary functions like heart rate and digestion and operates without your conscious input. The ANS divides further into:

THE SYMPATHETIC NERVOUS SYSTEM:
This system activates the "fight-or-flight" response, preparing the body for action.

THE PARASYMPATHETIC NERVOUS SYSTEM:
This is the "rest-and-digest" system, and it helps the body calm down and conserve energy.

Some also refer to a third component, the enteric nervous system (ENS), which governs the functions of the gastrointestinal system and operates semi-independently of the other branches. But in the context of stress and regulation, we'll focus on the ANS. It's there, in the interplay between sympathetic and parasympathetic responses, that your body decides whether to gear up for action or wind down. Understanding and managing this dynamic, particularly in sensitive nervous systems, is crucial in shaping your experiences and responses to the world.

Visualizing the Whole Nervous System

THE HUMAN NERVOUS SYSTEM

CENTRAL NERVOUS SYSTEM

The command center

PERIPHERAL NERVOUS SYSTEM

The messengers, sending signals to and from the brain and body

AUTONOMIC NERVOUS SYSTEM

INVOLUNTARY

This system controls breath rate, heart rate, and other automatic processes.

SOMATIC NERVOUS SYSTEM

VOLUNTARY

This system involves voluntary action and coordinates movement.

Stress responses, much like sneezes, are mostly out of our control (involuntary). However, we can influence our reactions once they occur. Recognizing their automatic nature can help in reducing the shame tied to our intense stress reactions.

When we talk about "the nervous system" in relation to stress, we're typically referring to the autonomic nervous system.

Sympathetic Nervous System

This system is responsible for mobilizing the body for action. It is what activates your fight-or-flight response during extreme stress.

Parasympathetic Nervous System

This system calms your body and aids the rest-and-digest process.

Your Sympathetic Nervous System in Action

Fight-or-Flight Mode
The body's natural response to threat

The sympathetic nervous system is the driver behind your fight-or-flight response, and it triggers a cascade of physiological changes when you perceive a threat, which helps your body prioritize immediate survival needs. For example, your:

- *Pupils dilate so you can take in more information.*
- *Heartbeat accelerates.*
- *Airways relax so you can take in more air.*
- *Stomach activity is slowed in order to redirect blood flow to your limbs and muscles to prepare you for rapid action.*
- *Intestinal and gallbladder activity are inhibited.*
- *Body secretes epinephrine and norepinephrine, hormones that help mobilize it for action by increasing heart rate, blood pressure, and energy levels.*
- *Sweat glands stimulate secretions to help cool the body as it prepares for rapid physical action.*

While these physiological changes primed our ancestors for survival, in today's world, they often appear in less physically demanding yet still very emotionally taxing situations. This misalignment between ancient responses and modern-day stressors can profoundly affect your behavior and emotions. For instance, the adrenaline rush meant to fuel a quick escape or a fierce confrontation can instead heighten anxiety or prompt overreaction in social or work settings, where such responses are not only unnecessary but often detrimental.

These responses happen because your body doesn't differentiate between an ancient threat and contemporary stressors. It interprets stress uniformly, meaning that your physiological reactions are the same whether you're facing life-threatening danger or navigating the stresses of homework, job responsibilities, parenting, or maintaining friendships.

And when your fight-or-flight system is activated too frequently due to your body's misinterpretation of stressors, it can cause problems. Once you learn to recognize the signs of sympathetic activation, you can employ practices such as deep breathing or physical activity to help recalibrate your body's reaction, steering you away from unnecessary hyperarousal.

Your Parasympathetic Nervous System in Action

Rest-and-Digest Mode

Aids our bodies' restoration, rest, and basic functions (digestion, etc.)

The parasympathetic nervous system is responsible for the rest-and-digest mode, signaling to your body that it is in a state of safety, where it can afford to shift its focus back to the essential maintenance activities that were put on hold during times of stress. In this mode, your body understands it's time to prioritize the vital processes of digesting food; engaging in deep, restorative sleep; and embracing a state of relaxation and recovery. In addition, your:

- *Pupils constrict.*
- *Heartbeat slows.*
- *Airways constrict.*
- *Stomach activity is stimulated.*
- *Intestinal and gallbladder activity are stimulated.*

This division of the autonomic nervous system acts as a counterbalance to the sympathetic nervous system's fight-or-flight response. It's your body's natural way of conserving energy and replenishing resources after periods of stress or activity.

Moreover, the parasympathetic nervous system is instrumental in regulating your mood, and it has a calming effect on your emotional state. By reducing stress levels and promoting relaxation, it helps to mitigate the negative impacts of chronic stress and anxiety on your health. Engaging this restful state not only supports physical health but also enhances mental well-being, encouraging a peaceful mind and a more resilient stress-response system.

Lifestyle choices, including balanced nutrition, regular physical activity, and healthy sleep patterns, play a significant role in supporting the parasympathetic nervous system's functions, enhancing your overall ability to relax and recover from stress. In addition, understanding how to consciously engage and strengthen your parasympathetic nervous system—through practices such as mindfulness, deep breathing exercises, and relaxation techniques—can empower you to better manage stress.

Your Vagus Nerve in Action

The "Wandering Nerve"
Latin word "vagus" meaning "wandering"

The vagus nerve, often called the "wandering nerve," is crucial for keeping our bodies relaxed and balanced. It's part of the parasympathetic nervous system, which helps us rest, digest, and recover. The vagus nerve travels throughout the body, connecting to major organs and influencing things like heart rate, digestion, and breathing.

The health of your **vagus nerve** is often measured by something called **vagal tone**. Having good vagal tone is like having a well-tuned nervous system. It means you can bounce back from stress more easily, keeping yourself calm and balanced as you address incoming stressors.

Autistic people often have lower vagal tone, which is why I describe the Autistic nervous system as "rigid." This means your nervous system may be more reactive than others, making it harder to stay calm and regulated. However, with the right practices, you can work on improving your vagal tone and increasing your nervous system resilience.

If you've judged yourself for having "big reactions," you're not alone. Have you noticed that you react more strongly to stress than others? If so, what stories have you told yourself about it? For example, have you thought, "I'm too sensitive," "I'm overreacting," or "I should be tougher"? Reflect on those narratives in the space here.

A Healthy Nervous System Is Flexible

Finding Balance in Your Nervous System

Ideally, your sympathetic and parasympathetic nervous systems work together seamlessly to maintain balance, also called your body's state of "homeostasis." It's a common misconception to view the sympathetic nervous system as inherently bad and the parasympathetic as solely good; the reality is more nuanced. A robust nervous system is a flexible nervous system—and both branches play important roles in keeping you healthy and responsive to life's demands.

For a grossly oversimplified yet sticky metaphor of the nervous system, imagine it as a car. The sympathetic system is the gas pedal, giving you energy, while the parasympathetic system is the brakes, helping you slow down and recover. Having a well-functioning nervous system is like driving a smooth, modern car that knows when to accelerate and brake. But if your nervous system is more rigid, it's like driving a 1970s truck with a sticky brake pedal through rough terrain—meanwhile, others seem to effortlessly glide through life, and you wonder why you struggle to keep up. It's because they are driving luxury sedans while you're driving the 1970s truck with a stick shift and unreliable brakes!

Strengthen Your Vagal Tone

Certain practices can stimulate the vagus nerve, which helps boost vagal tone. For example:

Deep, slow breathing exercises

Gentle yoga

Singing or humming

Sleep, nutrition, and movement

The Window of Tolerance

The "window of tolerance," introduced by Dr. Dan Siegel, is the optimal zone where you can effectively manage emotions and stress. Within this zone, known as the "optimal arousal" range, individuals can stay balanced and respond to challenges without becoming overwhelmed. However, everyone has a different-sized window of tolerance. Some people (those driving luxury sedan nervous systems!) can handle a large amount of stress before entering a dysregulated state, while others have a narrower window.

External pressures such as stress, intense emotions, and overstimulating sensory environments can thrust you out of your window of tolerance. Once you exceed this zone, your reactions tend to go in one of two directions:

1 A state of **HYPERAROUSAL**, which is driven by the sympathetic nervous system's fight-or-flight response

2 A state of **HYPOAROUSAL**, where your system essentially shuts down in an attempt to cope

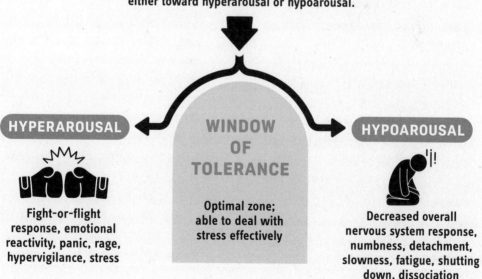

STRESS

There are two places outside the window of tolerance:
either toward hyperarousal or hypoarousal.

HYPERAROUSAL

Fight-or-flight response, emotional reactivity, panic, rage, hypervigilance, stress

WINDOW OF TOLERANCE

Optimal zone; able to deal with stress effectively

HYPOAROUSAL

Decreased overall nervous system response, numbness, detachment, slowness, fatigue, shutting down, dissociation

What Does Hyperarousal Look Like?

While your stress responses can vary based on different factors, many people have a consistent pattern. For example, I often shut down (hypoarousal) in response to sensory stress, while perceived mistakes or rejection push me into hyperarousal. Understanding your stress patterns helps you recognize when you're tipping into hyperarousal or hypoarousal, giving you more control to gently guide yourself back into your window of tolerance. Use the checklists here and on the following pages to identify your stress patterns.

HYPERAROUSAL: State of Mobilization

During hyperarousal, the body is gearing up for danger. The body responds by releasing adrenaline and cortisol and energizing the body to flee or fight.

 HYPERAROUSAL CHECKLIST

Review this checklist and consider how often these responses show up for you. Check off any that you've experienced before.

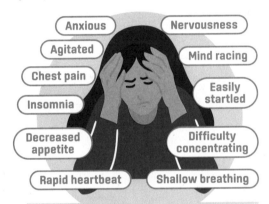

- **AGITATION:** Feeling restless, tense, or easily annoyed

- **REVVING UP:** Experiencing an adrenaline rush or heightened energy

- **PANIC:** Intense fear or anxiety that feels overwhelming

- **WORRY AND RACING THOUGHTS:** Persistent, uncontrollable anxious thoughts

- **HYPERVIGILANCE:** Being overly aware and on alert for potential threats

- **DIFFICULTY CONCENTRATING:** Struggling to focus on tasks

- **DIFFICULTY SHUTTING DOWN:** Trouble relaxing or sleeping

- **PHYSICAL SENSATIONS OF AROUSAL:** Chest pain, rapid heartbeat, or shallow breathing

Several conditions are often associated with "sympathetic dominance." When people experience the following conditions (note—this is not an exhaustive list), their nervous systems are often functioning in a sympathetic-dominant mode:

- Anxiety disorders, OCD, and phobic disorders
- PTSD and complex PTSD (C-PTSD)
- Borderline, histrionic, and paranoid personality disorders
- Manic episodes

What Does Hypoarousal Look Like?

HYPOAROUSAL: When Things Shut Down

During the state of hypoarousal, the body is attempting to protect itself from stress by shutting down in an attempt to take in or experience less of the stress.

 HYPOAROUSAL CHECKLIST

Review this checklist and consider how often these responses show up for you. Check off any that you've experienced before.

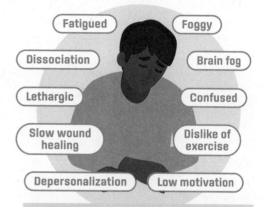

- **NUMBNESS:** Feeling emotionally or physically numb, as though your senses are dulled

- **DISCONNECTION:** Experiencing a sense of detachment from your surroundings or yourself

- **FATIGUE:** Feeling exhausted or having low energy, even after rest

- **FOGGY THINKING:** Struggling with clarity of thought, memory, or concentration

- **DEREALIZATION:** Perceiving the world around you as unreal or dreamlike

- **DEPERSONALIZATION:** Feeling disconnected from your own body or as if you're observing yourself from outside

- **HELPLESSNESS:** Feeling overwhelmed and unable to take action

- **APATHY:** A lack of interest or motivation in activities that normally engage you

The following conditions, among others, are often associated with the nervous system being in a chronic or prolonged state of hypoarousal:

- Depression
- Schizoid and schizotypal personality disorders
- PTSD and complex PTSD (C-PTSD) with a dissociated hypoarousal profile

Recognizing Your Window of Tolerance

It's also helpful to recognize what it feels like when you're in your window of tolerance. In this optimal zone of arousal, you can be the most present, engaged, and focused, allowing you to respond to incoming stressors with a sense of agency.

WINDOW OF TOLERANCE: When Things Are Working Smoothly

When you're in your window of tolerance, you are at an optimal level of arousal where you can effectively manage life tasks, emotions, and stressors.

 WINDOW OF TOLERANCE CHECKLIST

Review this checklist and consider how often these responses show up for you. Check off any that you've experienced before.

- Present and aware
- Engaged with tasks and people
- Clearheaded and focused
- Emotionally balanced
- Able to respond thoughtfully rather than reactively
- Feeling grounded and connected to your body
- Energy levels stable and steady
- Open to experiencing a range of emotions without feeling overwhelmed
- Creativity flowing naturally and problem-solving feeling achievable
- Able to access executive functioning skills and engage in play and creativity

Those with a larger window of tolerance can handle more arousal and stress before becoming dysregulated. Several factors contribute to a narrowing of the window of tolerance, including:

- Trauma and adverse life experiences
- Sensitive temperament
- Being Autistic (due to our sensitive nervous systems)
- Chronic stress
- Medical conditions
- Lifestyle factors (poor sleep, nutrient deficiencies, lack of movement)

What Size Is Your Window?

For many Autistic people, the window of tolerance tends to be quite narrow! In fact, many of us might find it challenging to even articulate what our window of tolerance feels like, given how infrequently we find ourselves within this zone of equilibrium.

Viewing your experiences through the lens of this metaphor can help you foster a deeper sense of empathy toward yourself, especially in moments when you might "overreact" or experience a meltdown. It's a gentle reminder that most people operate with a significantly larger window of tolerance and are equipped to absorb a greater onslaught of stressors before their systems tip into states of distress. I have found this perspective can be incredibly validating, helping us understand and extend kindness to ourselves—we are not simply "overreacting"; we're working with a much more sensitive (and narrow) system.

When your window of tolerance is small, your nervous system may look something like this:

HYPERAROUSAL

WINDOW OF TOLERANCE

HYPOAROUSAL

On the other hand, some people have a higher threshold for stress, and their nervous systems would look more like this:

HYPERAROUSAL

WINDOW OF TOLERANCE

HYPOAROUSAL

Use the space here to draw or visually represent your window of tolerance. Consider whether it feels more narrow or wider (you can refer back to your checklists to gauge this).

How to Increase Your Window of Tolerance

The good news is that your nervous system—even if it's more sensitive and characterized by a narrower window of tolerance—isn't fixed in its capacity. You can expand your window of tolerance by enhancing your vagal tone, processing old wounds, and cultivating more awareness of your nervous system states.

Practices such as mindfulness, movement, relaxation, and nervous system tracking offer effective paths toward this goal. However, nervous system healing also involves deeper work—processing old traumas, attachment wounds, and internalized ableism. It's important to keep in mind that nervous system "hacks" can't replace the deeper work of healing. The process of healing and nurturing your nervous system is gradual; be gentle and patient with yourself as you take this on!

Practices That Increase the Window of Tolerance

Here are some ideas of things you can do to enlarge your window of tolerance. Check off the ones that interest you, and add your own ideas or additional thoughts in the blank spaces.

Exposure to nature (even just seeing it out your window) can activate the parasympathetic nervous system and improve stress recovery.

Processing and releasing old wounds and traumas via tools like journaling can have a positive impact. Working with a trauma therapist can be beneficial.

Healing attachment wounds can reduce related triggers and enhance nervous system resilience. Insecure attachment often leads to emotional triggers and increased stress within the nervous system. Working with a relational or attachment-based therapist can be particularly beneficial in this process.

Creative expression can help by allowing you to process and express emotions in a nonspoken, often less threatening way.

Vagal nerve stimulation through methods such as breath work, vagal nerve stimulators (devices like the Sensate), humming, and chanting as well as working with someone who does craniosacral therapy or body work can be very helpful.

Movement can help you release stress and complete the stress cycle, which helps improve vagal tone.

Engaging in connection with others, including coregulation with pets, helps to calm the nervous system as it links up with another's regulated system, promoting a sense of safety and security.

Making sure all your biological needs are met (for example, eating nutrient-dense food, getting enough sleep, engaging in physical movement, and addressing inflammation) is a vital component in managing your window of tolerance.

Knowing what tends to trigger stress and engaging in mindful ways of unhooking from these triggers can help you build resilience.

Getting to know your nervous system and practice upregulating and downregulating can help you return to your window of tolerance.

"Mapping" Your Nervous System
TO HELP MANAGE IT

Nervous system mapping, widely used in trauma-informed practices, is a powerful tool for understanding where you are in your nervous system. Originally developed to help people with trauma better locate their stress responses, it's especially empowering for Autistic individuals, many of whom have experienced nervous system trauma. By helping you identify whether you're in a state of hyperarousal (fight-or-flight) or hypoarousal (shutdown), this practice guides you to find balance within your window of tolerance.

With nervous system mapping, you're acting like a detective for your own body, identifying the signs and patterns that reveal how you naturally respond to stress and stimuli. This self-awareness empowers you to better manage stress and find balance.

Mapping your nervous system includes two steps:

1 Locating what state you're in at any given moment

2 Identifying both your triggers and what's called "glimmers" (which are helpful things that bring you back to your window of tolerance)

At its heart, nervous system mapping is about tuning into your body's signals and reactions. It helps you gain a clearer understanding of your internal states, guiding you toward better self-attunement and care. Because to train your nervous system, you first need to know how to track it.

While nervous system mapping was initially developed from polyvagal theory, grounded in the work of Dr. Stephen Porges and expanded by practitioners like Deb Dana and Dr. Peter Levine, I've adapted it to focus on neurobiological principles more widely accepted in the scientific community, acknowledging the ongoing debate around polyvagal theory. The nervous system term "glimmers" was coined by Deb Dana.

MAP IT OUT, STEP ONE

Track Your State

The first step in gaining agency over your body is knowing where you are in your nervous system and locating yourself moment to moment. To do that, think about your feelings, thoughts, behaviors, physical sensations, and view of the world when you're in each state. Here's an example to get you started.

HYPERAROUSAL

FEELINGS:	*Irritable, angry, anxious, agitated*
THOUGHTS:	*"I just want to get out of here," "Make it stop"*
BEHAVIORS:	*More likely to yell or react quickly*
PHYSICAL SENSATIONS:	*Heart racing, jittery energy, heat*
VIEW OF THE WORLD:	*All-or-nothing and urgent thinking—everything feeling either all bad or demanding immediate attention, seeming catastrophic*

TIP: Essentially, you want to discover your "tells," which indicate that you are in a stressed state. Many Autistic people have alexithymia, where it is hard to discern our emotions. If that describes you, you should focus less on feelings and more on behaviors, thoughts, or things that feel more concrete to you.

WINDOW OF TOLERANCE

FEELINGS:	*Energetic, creative, calm, happy, mellow*
THOUGHTS:	*"I've got this," lots of ideation (playing with ideas)*
BEHAVIORS:	*More social, will often get started on a new creative project*
PHYSICAL SENSATIONS:	*A sense of physical presence and grounding, with energy that feels balanced, not overwhelming.*
VIEW OF THE WORLD:	*Hopeful and balanced, open to new experiences, and positive about the future*

TIP: If you struggle to identify what this feels like, think about how your body and/or mind feel when you are deeply focused on an area of interest.

HYPOAROUSAL

FEELINGS:	*Foggy, disconnected, exhausted, thick*
THOUGHTS:	*"I want to sleep," "I feel disconnected"*
BEHAVIORS:	*Shutdown, speaking difficulty, noninteractive*
PHYSICAL SENSATIONS:	*Tired, body feeling heavy and sluggish*
VIEW OF THE WORLD:	*Apathetic, with a sense of "What's the point?"*

TIP: It's possible you have distinct triggers for hyperarousal or hypoarousal states. For example, I've observed that certain sensory inputs, like large crowds, tend to induce a shutdown mode for me, whereas dealing with technology in public settings often leads to a hyperarousal state. However, your triggers might not be exclusively linked to one particular stress response.

AVAILABLE FOR DOWNLOAD

Track Your State

Now it's your turn. Try to fill in each section, but feel free to just skip any that you don't have a solid answer to.

HYPERAROUSAL

FEELINGS:	
THOUGHTS:	
BEHAVIORS:	
PHYSICAL SENSATIONS:	
VIEW OF THE WORLD:	

WINDOW OF TOLERANCE

FEELINGS:	
THOUGHTS:	
BEHAVIORS:	
PHYSICAL SENSATIONS:	
VIEW OF THE WORLD:	

HYPOAROUSAL

FEELINGS:	
THOUGHTS:	
BEHAVIORS:	
PHYSICAL SENSATIONS:	
VIEW OF THE WORLD:	

MAP IT OUT, STEP TWO

Know Your Triggers and Glimmers

Now that you can locate where you are in your nervous system, the second step is to identify your common triggers and your nervous system helpers, often referred to as glimmers. To do that, think about your physical, emotional, and relational states when you're in each phase. These examples might help spark some ideas.

HYPERAROUSAL	⚠ TRIGGERS ⚠
PHYSICAL:	Heat, discomfort, being around irritating sounds
EMOTIONAL:	Hot emotions such as anger, irritation, and embarrassment
RELATIONAL:	Feeling taken advantage of or abandoned or rejected

WINDOW OF TOLERANCE	✦ GLIMMERS ✦
PHYSICAL:	Soothing, repetitive movement (skating, basketball, running)
EMOTIONAL:	Doing activities that bring feelings of accomplishment or creativity
RELATIONAL:	Connecting deeply with a friend

HYPOAROUSAL	⚠ TRIGGERS ⚠
PHYSICAL:	Too much going on around me (too many bodies, too much sound)
EMOTIONAL:	Sadness, overwhelm, shame
RELATIONAL:	During emotionally intense conversations or when people are mad

The terms "triggers" and "glimmers" are derived from the work of Deb Dana. However, in this context, they are used with a broader neurobiological focus rather than drawing strictly from polyvagal theory.

Know Your Triggers and Glimmers

Here's space for you to write your own answers in the spaces provided.

AVAILABLE FOR DOWNLOAD

HYPERAROUSAL ⚠ TRIGGERS ⚠

PHYSICAL:

EMOTIONAL:

RELATIONAL:

WINDOW OF TOLERANCE ★ GLIMMERS ★

PHYSICAL:

EMOTIONAL:

RELATIONAL:

HYPOAROUSAL ⚠ TRIGGERS ⚠

PHYSICAL:

EMOTIONAL:

RELATIONAL:

Pitfalls to Avoid While Tracking Your Nervous System

Understanding how to track your nervous system sets the stage for effectively training it. This involves gently guiding it back to the window of tolerance when you detect a stressed state. Before delving into how to do that, though, it's important to highlight two common pitfalls Autistic people might encounter when beginning to track our nervous systems.

PITFALL #1

Judging Your Stress Levels

When you start to track your nervous system, you'll likely become more aware of your stress states. However, this newfound awareness can lead you into the trap of judging your stress levels. Thoughts like "Oh no, I'm stressed or overwhelmed, this is bad, I need to return to a calm state" can actually *heighten* your stress, creating a secondary layer of stress about being stressed. This cycle can cause constriction (a tightening or narrowing of your physical or emotional state in response to stress), keeping you stuck in that stressed state instead of helping to release it.

PITFALL #2

Forced Attempts to Shift

The second pitfall is that when you recognize a stressed state, your instinct might be to forcefully regulate it, either by trying to calm down or ramping up too abruptly. Approaching your nervous system with an attitude of fear, panic, or force and attempting to immediately "fix" it leads to increased stress and often backfires. Even something that seems helpful, like telling yourself, "I must take three deep breaths right now!" can introduce tension and worsen the stress. This approach can prevent the natural, gentle return to a state of balance.

Try to Expand, Accept, Acknowledge, and Care

So, if judging and forcing *aren't* the paths forward, what should you do instead? The answer lies in expansion and agency—welcoming the experience by accepting and acknowledging it as it is, thereby creating space for its presence. This approach involves being present to the experience and, from a space of nonjudgmental awareness, deciding how you want to respond. By making choices from a place of agency, you can move forward with self-care, whether that's through relaxation practices, grounding techniques, or distraction. The key is to engage with these practices intentionally, allowing yourself to navigate your emotions and reactions in a measured way.

The following question prompts are designed to facilitate this expansive and gentle energy, enabling you to compassionately accompany your nervous system back to a state of safety.

A Questions to Foster Expansion and Acceptance

Acceptance acts as a bridge from constriction to openness. Here are some questions to ask yourself to see if you're open to expanding into this moment.

Can I make space for this experience right now?

_____

_____

_____

Can I allow myself to be exactly as I am in this moment, without needing to change anything?

_____

_____

_____

Am I willing to simply notice and be with this sensation even if just for a moment?

_____

_____

_____

Can I acknowledge this experience without attaching a story or judgment to it?

_____

_____

_____

B Questions to Foster Acknowledgment and Gain Self-Insight

Stress within your nervous system can serve as both a reminder and an invitation. You might think of it as an alarm that's alerting you to unmet needs and a call toward deeper self-understanding. The following questions are designed to guide you toward uncovering insights about your needs and feelings.

What is this sensation telling me about my current boundaries and limits?

_____

_____

_____

What unmet need might my stress be trying to tell me about?

_____

_____

_____

What is my stress teaching me about my current state or desires?

_____

_____

_____

C Questions for Boosting Self-Care Through Gentle Inquiry

In moments of stress, turning toward yourself with kindness can transform your experience. The questions here aim to guide you toward nurturing practices. They encourage a pause for reflection, inviting a softer, more compassionate approach to your current state.

In what small way can I comfort or care for myself right now?

_____

_____

_____

_____

What do I need in this moment?

_____

_____

_____

How is my breathing right now, and can I gently invite it to slow down?

_____

_____

_____

_____

What would happen if I approached myself with curiosity instead of criticism?

_____

_____

_____

The Basics of Nervous System State Shifting

Now that you have gained clarity on the ideal attitude to have toward your nervous system, you can start practicing nervous system state shifting. This involves intentionally engaging in activities to adjust the state of your nervous system. The steps to do this are:

1

Recognize your current state.

2

If you're predominantly in a
SYMPATHETIC (HIGH AROUSAL) STATE,
consider **DOWNREGULATING ACTIVITIES**.

If you're experiencing
IMMOBILIZATION (LOW AROUSAL), think about
incorporating **UPREGULATING PRACTICES**.

It's important to note that as stress responses can be protective and necessary in situations of real danger—providing the extra energy required for self-defense—the concept of state shifting primarily applies to nonthreatening situations where you do not need immediate physical protection.

ACTIVITIES TO DOWNREGULATE: Downregulating involves decreasing the body's arousal and activation levels, beneficial for calming an overly stimulated state.

Progressive muscle relaxation

Breath work

Yoga
(be mindful that some yoga is upregulating so look for positions like Child's Pose that activate your relaxation response)

Ideas for Downregulating/Calming Activities

On this page and a following one are lists of activities designed to either calm or energize you. As you explore these suggestions, check any that appeal to you, and add your own suggestions in the blank spaces provided. These lists are adapted from "Sensory Approaches" by Dr. Tina Champagne. You can find the original list here: https://mass.gov/doc/sensory-approaches/download.

Everyone's sensory system is unique—what soothes one person might not have the same effect on another. Approach these options with an open mind, consider trying some out if you haven't already, and closely observe how your body reacts. This process is about discovering what specifically aligns with your sensory state and arousal needs.

ENVIRONMENTAL ADJUSTMENTS

○ *Opt for warm, soft lighting to create a cozy atmosphere.*
○ *Choose environments with mild stimuli and few, subtle colors to reduce sensory overload.*
○ *Prioritize familiar settings at a slow pace to foster a sense of security and calm.*
○ *Use soft materials or textures like a cozy blanket or plush pillow.*

PERSONAL ACTIVITIES

○ *Engage in slow, rhythmic activities like rocking in a chair to soothe the body.*
○ *Use deep pressure or weighted blankets for a comforting sense of grounding.*
○ *Listen to mellow music or ambient sounds to calm the mind.*
○ *Sip warm beverages or practice aromatherapy with mild scents for sensory comfort.*
○ *Take a warm shower or bath.*
○ *Hum, chant, or sing to activate the vagus nerve.*
○ *Practice downregulating yoga positions.*
○ *Explore green therapy (time in nature).*
○ *Try progressive muscle relaxation.*
○ *Practice slow breathing.*

ACTIVITIES TO UPREGULATE: Upregulating boosts your body's energy, alertness, and arousal levels, aiding in overcoming states of immobilization.

Rapid breath work

Lifting weights

Listening to upbeat music

Engaging in a stimulating activity

Taking a brisk walk

Exposing yourself to sunlight

Gentle stretching

Ideas for Upregulating/Energizing Activities

ENVIRONMENTAL ADJUSTMENTS

○ *Introduce bright colors and dynamic lighting to invigorate the space.*

○ *Seek out novel and stimulating environments or adjust your current setting for increased alertness.*

○ *Sit in a cool room or near a fan with airflow.*

PERSONAL ACTIVITIES

○ *Participate in fast, energetic movements like dancing, aerobic exercises, or a brisk outdoor walk to boost energy.*

○ *Experience strong flavors such as sour candies, lemon wedges, or spicy foods.*

○ *Use alerting scents like peppermint oil for sensory awakening.*

○ *Refresh and invigorate your senses with cold stimuli—take a cold shower, splash water on your face, use cold compresses, or stand in front of a fan.*

○ *Enjoy a frozen treat or crunching on ice cubes.*

○ *Stimulate focus and awaken the senses with dynamic visual stimuli— browse an I Spy book, enjoy the fluid motion of visual water toys, or watch a lava lamp.*

○ *Listen to fast-paced music.*

○ *Touch rough or prickly textures.*

○ *Do a few jumping jacks.*

○ *Practice rapid breath work.*

WHAT IS THE

Stress Cycle?

The concept of completing the stress cycle originates from the work of A.Z. Reznick, a biochemist, and was further developed by Dr. Peter Levine and other trauma specialists. It gained wider recognition through Drs. Emily and Amelia Nagoski in their book *Burnout.* Here's a visual representation of the stress cycle.

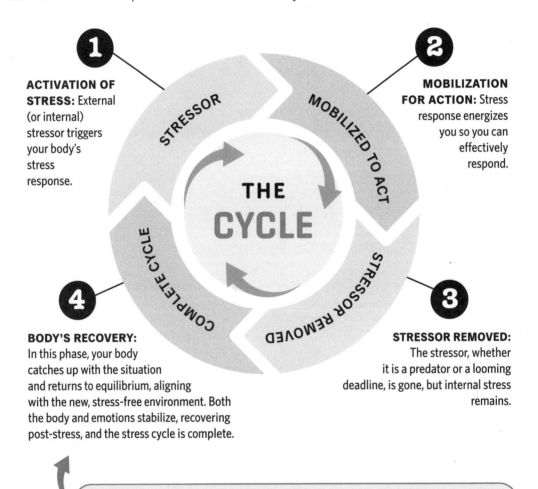

1

ACTIVATION OF STRESS: External (or internal) stressor triggers your body's stress response.

2

MOBILIZATION FOR ACTION: Stress response energizes you so you can effectively respond.

4

BODY'S RECOVERY: In this phase, your body catches up with the situation and returns to equilibrium, aligning with the new, stress-free environment. Both the body and emotions stabilize, recovering post-stress, and the stress cycle is complete.

3

STRESSOR REMOVED: The stressor, whether it is a predator or a looming deadline, is gone, but internal stress remains.

STRESSOR

MOBILIZED TO ACT

STRESSOR REMOVED

COMPLETE CYCLE

THE CYCLE

By completing the stress cycle, you inform your body that it is safe to return to a state of equilibrium, signaling that the immediate stressor has been addressed or is manageable. With chronic stressors, completing the stress cycle is essential for your well-being, even if the stressors persist and never really disappear. Understanding the distinction between the stress (your body's response) and the stressor (the external cause) is key to effective stress management.

The Importance of Completing the Stress Cycle

Now that you've got an overall sense of the stress cycle, let's examine it a bit more deeply. **Your body needs to complete this cycle after encountering a stressor to return to a state of balance.** In the wild, animals instinctively complete their stress cycles through physical actions, such as shaking off stress after a narrow escape, naturally allowing their bodies to release the stress.

In modern life, however, **completing the stress cycle often requires deliberate effort**, as your stressors can be both immediate and ongoing, and they can lack the physical resolution seen in nature. Yet modern stressors—like work demands or daily pressures—still elicit similar physiological responses as physical threats, potentially leaving you in a prolonged state of heightened alertness or a frozen stress state. Staying in these states can contribute to Autistic burnout.

Since you may not have a physical resolution (for example, escaping the predator), **you can intentionally signal to your body that a stressor has been addressed or is within your capacity to manage**, enabling you to return to a state of equilibrium. Importantly, you can address and move through the stress cycle even when the stressor remains present—in fact, this is a common necessity in modern life.

Our bodies require assistance to navigate this cycle. In *Burnout*, the Nagoski sisters explain that there is a difference between a stressor (the cause) and stress (the body's response). Your body can remain in a state of stress even after the stressor is gone, or you may face chronic stressors that require ongoing management. Learning to address the stress itself, rather than conflating it with the stressor, is key to effective stress management.

Ways to Complete the Stress Cycle

Movement, progressive muscle relaxation, and breathing are some of the most effective methods for completing the stress cycle. In *Burnout*, the Nagoski sisters suggest that everyone dedicate twenty minutes daily to this practice. I believe this advice is especially crucial for Autistic people, given the unique challenges we face with stress and sensory processing. Review these suggestions, and circle any that might work for you. Add your own ideas at the bottom of the page.

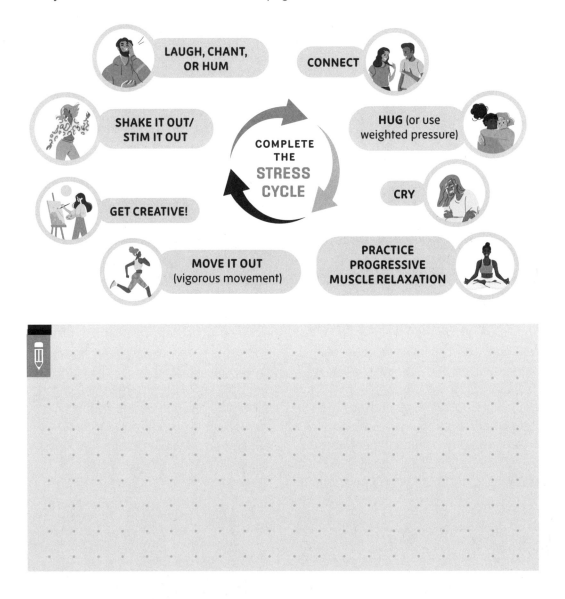

LAUGH, CHANT, OR HUM

CONNECT

SHAKE IT OUT/ STIM IT OUT

COMPLETE THE STRESS CYCLE

HUG (or use weighted pressure)

GET CREATIVE!

CRY

MOVE IT OUT (vigorous movement)

PRACTICE PROGRESSIVE MUSCLE RELAXATION

Deep Breathing Exercise

Deep breathing is a powerful tool to counter the fight-or-flight response because it activates your body's relaxation response. Especially during burnout, your body may remain in a state of prolonged stress, requiring additional support to complete the stress cycle. Deep breathing acts as a signal to your nervous system, indicating safety and assisting in navigating you through the stress cycle.

For effective slow, deep breathing, focus particularly on elongating your exhale. Additionally, placing a hand on your stomach can help ensure the breath is fully engaging the diaphragm and not shallowly filling the chest. Here's a simple deep breathing exercise you can try anytime, anywhere:

▶ Breathe in deeply through your nose for four seconds and hold for one second.

▶ Slowly release your breath out through your mouth for a count of six.

Notice how that breathing made you feel. Did it feel natural, or will it take some practice to feel comfortable? Did you notice any physical or emotional changes in your body after you completed the exercise? Is there an activity you do daily that you could start pairing this exercise with (for example, checking email)?

Progressive Muscle Relaxation Exercise

Progressive muscle relaxation is another powerful technique for activating your body's relaxation response, thereby aiding in the completion of the stress cycle. This method involves systematically tensing and then relaxing different muscle groups, a process that helps release built-up tension and promote overall relaxation. Activating intentional tension followed by relaxation not only eases physical stress but also signals to your nervous system that it is safe. Here's how to do it:

▶ Start with your feet and create tension by curling and tightening your toes. Hold for five seconds, then release. Repeat once more.

▶ Move to the next muscle group. You might want to move your way up your body, continuing from your feet to your calves, thighs, stomach, chest, arms, shoulders, neck, and face. You can finish by tensing and relaxing your whole body.

▶ I recommend listening to a recording that will walk you through the exercise the first time you do this.

Reflect on how this exercise made you feel. How did your muscles react to this process? Did it feel particularly good in any specific areas of your body? At what times in your life could you start using this exercise?

CHAPTER 5

Stabilizing Your Energy Using the Spoon Theory

Managing Energy Levels Is a Psychological Journey

Discovering I was Autistic brought me a profound sense of liberation, and yet, it also introduced some of the most challenging grief I've experienced—grieving my limits. These limits, spanning categories from energetic to sensory to relational, are often the hardest to accept and adapt to. In my work with Autistic people, I find this process of grieving our limits to be one of the areas where we struggle most. Here is the thing: **When you're Autistic, you need a lot of rest**! Like, an annoying amount of rest. And when we don't get that, our systems tend to shut down (hello, burnout!).

This chapter is perhaps the most important in this book, and it could be the hardest chapter for you to work through. The techniques in this chapter are actually *not* hard, but **coming to terms with your energy limits and learning to honor them is some of the hardest work of being Autistic**. We face both external challenges and internal struggles like grief and internalized ableism, which can hinder our ability to manage energy effectively. Before we dive into practical tools for energy management, it's important to first address these psychological barriers.

In this chapter, we will explore the "boom-or-bust" cycle of energy and learn about pacing systems, specifically the spoon theory. Keep in mind that although the ideas may seem straightforward, the real challenge lies in the psychological journey of accepting and implementing them. What lies on the other side of that acceptance is a world where you know how to anticipate your energy needs and replenish your energy levels.

Grieving Your Limits

After an autism diagnosis, many people do a lot of "clearing": We clear out old expectations, old items, old beliefs. Some of this clearing will feel liberating (like when I threw away all my lacy clothes and high-heeled shoes!). And some of this clearing will be hard and involve grief work. However, on the other side of that grieving is the liberation and freedom to accept what is.

> Clearing means that you let yourself **grieve the things that are different** from what you expected so that you can **appreciate what is**.

You might find yourself mourning and working to clear a variety of experiences— for example, you might have grief about decisions you've previously made (perhaps you fell into addiction or unhealthy relationship patterns while simply trying to survive), grief about the years you didn't know about your autism, or grief about your limits. To build a life that truly aligns with your needs, it is helpful to identify and work through these griefs.

THINGS I AM WORKING TO CLEAR
Use the space here to record anything you might be mourning.

WAYS TO PROCESS MY GRIEF
Check off any ideas that might work for you, and add your own in the blanks provided.

- ☐ Write a letter to my past or future self.
- ☐ Process in therapy or with a good friend.
- ☐ Identify the values under the grief. (For example, grieving Autistic limits might highlight a deep value in social connection or autonomy. Dr. Steven C. Hayes says we "hurt where we care," meaning our grief reveals our values. Identifying these values can help us understand the source of our pain and guide us in coping with it.)
- ☐ Engage in creative expression.

Addressing Internalized Ableism

"Internalized ableism" refers to the negative messages you've absorbed about your disability or about disabled people in general. One sneaky way this manifests is when you hold yourself to neurotypical standards and expect yourself to perform accordingly. These beliefs often cause you to push past your limits and ignore your need for rest. It's crucial to recognize and address these beliefs in order to properly manage your energy.

Examples of Thoughts Related to Internalized Ableism

Have you ever said any of these things to yourself? Check off the ones you've thought and add any others in the blank spaces.

○ "I just need to push through."
○ "This is simple. It shouldn't be so hard!"
○ "My friend can do this; I should be able to do this too."

○ "I just rested yesterday."
○ _____
○ _____

Exercises for Working Through Internalized Ableism

● **Talk to yourself as you would talk to a friend.**
  ▪ Consider what you would say to a friend who expressed similar thoughts.
  ▪ Write down your compassionate responses, then apply them to yourself.

● **Identify the core beliefs in your ableist statements.**
  ▪ Look for "should" statements in your thoughts, like "I should be able to do this."
  ▪ Reflect on why you feel pressured to meet these expectations. For instance, a core belief might be that being hardworking is essential to your worth, and when you struggle to meet those expectations, you may label yourself as "lazy" and "worthless."

● **Identify the core fear in your ableist statements.**
  ▪ Determine the underlying fear in your negative thought.
  ▪ Name this fear to understand its influence and consider how to address it. For example, you might fear being seen as unlovable if you don't meet certain expectations. Recognizing this fear can help you understand the driver behind your efforts and find ways to manage it.

Understanding the Boom-and-Bust Energy Cycle

The boom-and-bust cycle, which is common among people with disabilities or chronic illnesses, involves overextending yourself and then experiencing a significant energy crash. While healthy individuals may recover quickly, Autistic people and others with chronic conditions often take much longer to bounce back. On days when we have more energy or less pain, the urge to catch up on tasks can be overwhelming, leading us to ignore our bodies' signals and push past our limits.

The cycle goes like this:

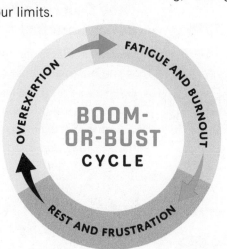

Why Is This Pattern Problematic?

This pattern becomes troublesome when it evolves into a lifestyle that drives you toward burnout. Here are a few of the problems associated with this cycle:

1 **IT DEMANDS A PROLONGED RECOVERY:** Each time you push yourself beyond your body's limits, recovery takes longer, deepening the burnout and exacerbating symptoms like chronic pain and fatigue.

2 **IT TAKES YOU ON AN EMOTIONAL ROLLER COASTER:** Your moods often mirror this cycle of energy expenditure and recovery, meaning that you experience periods of positivity and accomplishment during your "boom" days, followed by dips into sadness and disappointment during your "bust" days.

It's important to know that some degree of the boom-and-bust cycle is inevitable for neurodivergent people due to our interest-based nervous systems, all-or-nothing instincts, and capacity for hyperfocus. The goal isn't to eliminate this cycle completely, but to recognize it, understand it, and learn to work with it better.

What Are Pacing Systems?

A pacing system is a tool that helps you sustainably monitor and manage your energy. These systems lay out ways to distribute your energy more evenly throughout your days, reducing the severity of energy crashes. Here are some other benefits of pacing systems:

They Can Help You Navigate the Boom-and-Bust Roller Coaster

Several practices can gently ease you away from the highs and lows of the boom-and-bust cycle. These include addressing internalized ableism, setting respectful boundaries, and cultivating healthy sleep habits. Additionally, pacing systems can be a crucial aid in breaking this cycle. By integrating one or more of these strategies thoughtfully, you'll move toward a more balanced daily rhythm.

They Can Help You Manage Pain

My introduction to pacing systems came while working as a behavioral health provider in an oncology clinic, where I helped patients manage their energy and pain through careful pacing of activities. Pacing systems are invaluable in medical settings, especially for people dealing with chronic pain, fatigue, and other conditions associated with disabilities or chronic health issues.

They Can Give You Greater Control over Your Life

Pacing systems foster a more empowered lifestyle—increasing your sense of control, granting you greater agency over your daily activities, and reducing the feeling of being at the mercy of your body's fluctuating capacities.

Three Benefits of Pacing Systems for Autistic People

Anyone can use pacing systems, but I find that they are especially useful for Autistic people. Here are my top three reasons why:

They Are Tangible and Visual

Pacing systems transform abstract concepts like "energy" into tangible, visual elements that are particularly resonant for Autistic minds. Visual metaphors such as "spoons" or "energy units" provide concrete discussion anchors.

They Provide a Specific Vocabulary

These systems offer a specific language to discuss your needs, moving beyond the vague "I'm tired" to more precise expressions. By using terms like "energy units," you can clearly articulate your state to others, supporting effective communication and self-advocacy.

They Help Cultivate Self-Compassion

Pacing systems encourage regular, mindful self-check-ins. They prompt you to ask questions like: "How am I feeling right now?" "How much energy do I have?" "How demanding is this activity?" and "What do I need?" This practice of gentle self-assessment encourages you to regularly check in with your needs and be responsive to them.

Pacing Systems to Choose From

There are several different pacing systems out there. In this chapter, we'll be focusing on "spoon theory," as it's one of the most widely used in disability spaces. But if spoons don't resonate with you, you can either swap out "spoon" for another item or you could see if one of these alternative pacing systems might work better for you:

Traffic Light System

This method categorizes daily activities by energy demand: green for low energy (or energy-restoration activities), yellow for moderate, and red for high. By identifying activities in this way, you can spread out red light activities among plenty of yellow and green ones.

Energy Accounting

Created by Autistic advocate Maja Toudal, this approach treats energy like a bank account, balancing energy-intensive tasks ("withdrawals") with rest ("deposits") to avoid "overdrafts" and potential meltdowns. It involves listing activities—for example, you could assign energy costs on a 1–100 scale, then track your energy balance using those numbers.

Ticket Theory

Developed by Autistic YouTuber Hilary Knutson, this theory views daily tasks as carnival rides needing specific tickets. For example, a ticket for brushing your teeth can't be used for washing dishes, and if you don't use your homework ticket on time, you miss the chance to do it until you get another ticket. This model, including features like expiring tickets, highlights the challenges of executive functioning and interest-driven focus.

THE ORIGIN OF THE
Spoon Theory

The spoon theory was birthed in a diner where Christine Miserandino, now an award-winning writer, blogger, speaker, and lupus patient advocate, was having a meal with her college friend. Her friend inquired about what it was like to live with lupus, a chronic medical condition. After struggling to explain the medical details of lupus, Christine realized her friend was asking, "What does it *feel* like?"

At this point, Christine grabbed all the spoons at the table (and the ones nearby) and gave her friend a handful of spoons. She told her friend that most people wake up with an endless supply of spoons, but here, for this experiment, she would have twelve. She then asked her friend to walk her through her day, starting with waking up in the morning, listing each task she completed. Christine took a spoon from her friend for every single activity she listed (waking up, showering, getting dressed).

Christine used this metaphor to explain that when she woke up, she had a limited number of spoons and, therefore, had to meticulously think about every choice she made. Navigating life with a chronic illness meant she had to deliberately allocate her "spoons" to various activities throughout the day.

This metaphor is now widely used in the context of disability advocacy. It has become a powerful means for explaining how people grappling with chronic illness or fatigue must maintain a heightened awareness of their energy allocation. This concept is particularly helpful for those dealing with invisible disabilities, as it turns the invisible "visible" through the use of metaphor.

= **ENERGY UNIT**

How Many Spoons Do Your Tasks Require?

When people have energy limitations, they have a limited number of "spoons" they wake up with each morning. When your energy is limited, you must be more cautious in how you use it. You can monitor your energy daily by considering things such as:

> ▶ *How many spoons did I wake up with this morning?*
> ▶ *What activities are going to demand spoons from me today?*
> ▶ *How will I allocate my spoons today?*
> ▶ *Are there any activities that will recharge my supply of spoons?*

Different Activities Require Different Numbers of Spoons

Keep in mind that some activities demand more of your energy than others. Here are some common activities and how many spoons they might require. Of course, everyone's experience is different—showering may only be one spoon to you, while driving is three. In the following space, reflect on what are some of the high-spoon activities in your day.

It's also helpful to think about what puts spoons back in your jar—in other words, what activities can restore your energy levels. Later in this chapter, you will find space to consider what restores—and ignites—your energy.

The Neurodivergent-Specific Spoon Drawer

The concept of "spoons" as a metaphor for energy reserves can be somewhat vague for neurodivergent individuals, for whom energy distribution is not uniform across all activities. For instance, **you might have ample physical energy on a given day yet have limited capacity for tasks that demand high focus, or vice versa**. This complexity often leads to conflicting needs, such as having the desire to socialize ("social spoons") but being limited by sensory overload ("sensory spoons").

Recognizing these nuances, Autistic author and advocate Cynthia Kim advanced the spoon theory by suggesting a more tailored approach for Autistic people: different types of "spoons" for different functional areas—like mental energy, focus, or executive functioning.

An individual might lack the energy to go out to a restaurant with friends but have enough to engage in a solitary activity like reading or pursuing a special interest. This variability often leads to misunderstandings, with neurodivergent people being mislabeled as "lazy" or "selfish." For instance, a parent might challenge a child's claim of being too drained for chores if they are able to enjoy time with friends or indulge in a favorite book, because they haven't recognized that **different tasks require different types of energy, not just different amounts of energy**.

A useful tip for managing your diverse energy is to pair tasks that drain you with activities that refill your energy reserves. For example, I find that listening to a podcast about a topic I'm passionate about helps me stay energized while I tackle something more demanding, like cleaning.

SOURCE: Cynthia Kim, "Conserving Spoons," *Musings of an Aspie* (blog), October 15, 2014, https://musingsofanaspie.com/2014/10/15/conserving-spoons/.

Neurodivergent-Specific Spoon Types

Here is a list of different energy "spoons" for understanding daily energy management for Autistic people. Each category highlights a specific cognitive or physical demand. Please note, this is not an exhaustive list, and there may be additional types of spoons that impact you.

 EXECUTIVE FUNCTIONING (EF) SPOONS: *The cognitive resources required for tasks such as planning, organizing, focus, and decision-making*

 SOCIAL SPOONS: *Pertain to the energy needed for social interactions and communication and language-based communication*

 SENSORY SPOONS: *Encompass the capacity to manage sensory input and processing*

 PHYSICAL ENERGY SPOONS: *Represent the available physical stamina and vitality for various activities*

In addition to these four main types of neurodivergent spoons, you might want to create your own categories. For example, you might include **Language Spoons** (energy for communication), **Emotion Regulation Spoons** (resources to manage feelings), or **Adaptability Spoons** (bandwidth for shifting routines). If there's an area of your life that consistently uses energy, consider adding it to your "neurodivergent spoon drawer." Write down any additional categories here:

Take a Personalized Spoon Inventory

Now consider taking stock of your available spoons, focusing on the types most relevant to your daily life. You don't need to inventory every single type—doing so might be too demanding on your executive functioning spoons! For instance, I find that my EF, social, and physical energy spoons are the ones I need to monitor most closely on a day-to-day basis. When I wake up, I might have, say, ten EF spoons, four social spoons, and five physical energy spoons. Choose the categories that resonate most with your routine and energy-management needs.

EF SPOONS

.... *spoons*

.... *spoons*

SOCIAL SPOONS

SENSORY SPOONS

.... *spoons*

.... *spoons*

PHYSICAL ENERGY SPOONS

FILL IN YOUR OWN!

.... *spoons*

.... *spoons*

.... *spoons*

Energy Rhythms

An essential part of managing your energy is learning to recognize not only how many "spoons" you have on a given day but also **how your energy ebbs and flows throughout a day or week or even across seasons**. By tuning into these natural rhythms, you can begin to structure your tasks around times that best align with your energy flow.

For example, you might find you have your best **cognitive energy** in the morning, or, like me, you may feel the sharpest late at night (even when you should be sleeping!). Some people also experience **cyclical** or **seasonal** energy fluctuations, with periods of higher creativity during certain months and lower energy during others.

Understanding these patterns allows you to plan more effectively. In my case, I wrote most of this book in winter and spring. Knowing that winter is typically a lower-energy season for me, I took myself to California, where the environment better supported my energy. Similarly, I know my brain is foggy in the morning, so I schedule deep, focused tasks for the afternoon and evening when my cognitive energy is at its peak. On the next page is a series of reflection prompts to get you thinking about *your* different energy rhythms.

Embracing the *ebb and flow* of your neurodivergent energy is an *act of self-compassion*, honoring your natural rhythms and guiding you toward *greater alignment and balance*.

Take an Inventory of Your Energy Rhythms

Spend a few moments to reflect on your energy patterns
during different parts of the day and across seasons.

Daily Energy Patterns

MORNING: *How do you generally feel in the morning? Are you mentally sharp and physically energized, or do you feel sluggish? What types of tasks (if any) do you find easiest to complete in the morning?*

AFTERNOON: *How does your energy shift after midday? Do you notice a dip in focus, or do you hit your productivity stride? What types of tasks are easiest for you during this time?*

EVENING: *How do you feel as the day winds down? What tasks do you prefer to leave for the evening, if any?*

Seasonal Energy Patterns

HIGH-ENERGY SEASONS: *Do you notice certain months in which you feel more creative or productive? What types of projects do you typically take on during these times?*

LOW-ENERGY SEASONS: *Are there seasons in which your energy tends to drop or when you feel less motivated? How do you manage tasks during these periods?*

Match Your Tasks with Your Energy Levels

Now that you've assessed your available spoons across various domains and have an idea of your energy rhythms, the next step is to align your activities with your natural energy flows rather than fighting against them. For instance, I've noticed that trying to write an assessment report or engage in writing tasks when my executive functioning spoons are low not only proves inefficient but also drains a huge amount of energy. Instead, I now work with the current rather than against it. This approach has led to a somewhat unpredictable schedule—some weeks, my house is clean; other weeks, I accomplish a lot of writing or focus on design work.

While you may not always have the flexibility to perfectly match your tasks with your energy levels, making an effort to do so can significantly boost productivity, reduce frustration, and conserve energy. Trying to "power through" with low spoons often leads to major energy depletion. The following form can help you start thinking about how to best pair your activities with your spoon availability. Check out the example that's done for you, then fill in some of your own.

EXAMPLE

TASK: *Write a report for work*

SPOON TYPE NEEDED: *Executive functioning spoons*

BEST TIME SLOT: *Afternoons (2 p.m.–4 p.m., when EF spoons are at their peak)*

TASK:

SPOON TYPE NEEDED: | BEST TIME SLOT:

TASK:

SPOON TYPE NEEDED: | BEST TIME SLOT:

TASK:

SPOON TYPE NEEDED: | BEST TIME SLOT:

TASK:

SPOON TYPE NEEDED: | BEST TIME SLOT:

TASK:

SPOON TYPE NEEDED: | BEST TIME SLOT:

TASK:

SPOON TYPE NEEDED: | BEST TIME SLOT:

Plan Meaningful Low-Energy Activities

One of the most challenging aspects of burnout is the feeling of collapse, which can spiral into a lethargy cycle, which then perpetuates feelings of depression and lack of accomplishment. That's why it's crucial to have a reserve of low-energy activities that still foster a sense of **meaning** and **accomplishment**. Many Autistic people, including myself, find it stressful to "do nothing." While rest is essential during burnout, it's important not to fall into a *complete* inactivity trap.

For instance, if you find yourself with low social spoons but high EF spoons, it's the perfect time to turn on "do not disturb," find a quiet spot, and dive into some work projects. (Bonus: The monotropic flow state is deeply restorative for us.) On days when my energy is low, I can catch up on coursework, and when I feel more energetic, I tackle more demanding projects like reports or papers. The aim is to work in harmony with the spoons you have while honoring those you don't. So much of Autistic burnout recovery and resilience is about **learning to work with your natural rhythms versus forcing yourself into misaligned rhythms**.

Planning ahead of time for some meaningful activities you can do even when energy is low can be incredibly beneficial. Try to focus on activities that are **meaningful**, will provide a sense of **accomplishment**, or are **restorative**. Read over the examples here, then use the next page to fill in your own ideas.

★ EXAMPLE ★

 My Low Spoon Plan

Low Physical Energy Spoons	Low EF Spoons
On days I'm low on physical energy spoons, I can still enjoy . . .	On days I'm low on EF spoons, I can still enjoy . . .
▶ *Focusing on input (reading, listening to podcasts) rather than output*	▶ *Physical activities like a walk*
▶ *Resting or sitting outside for some fresh air*	▶ *Watching a favorite, comforting TV show*
▶ *Reading ahead for class*	▶ *Doing repetitive tasks (like laundry)*
	▶ *Catching up on light housework*

Now it's your turn. Pick the spoon categories that are most relevant to you, and write down some ideas for each one.

My Low Spoon Plan

LOW _____ SPOONS

LOW _____ SPOONS

LOW _____ SPOONS

LOW _____ SPOONS

LOW _____ SPOONS

LOW _____ SPOONS

UNDERSTANDING
Energy Igniters and Zappers

Finally, along with matching your energy to tasks, you might consider pinpointing your energy igniters and energy zappers. Both are important: When navigating the tricky terrain of burnout, discovering what recharges you is just as vital as figuring out what drains you. This igniters-and-zappers theme can fit into any pacing system you're using!

ENERGY IGNITERS

are those things that nourish and replenish you, give you a boost, and act like a jump-start. These activities or tools put spoons back in your drawer or dollars back in the bank—whichever energy metaphor resonates with you!

ENERGY ZAPPERS

are the pesky culprits that steal those precious spoons (or dollars, or whatever energy currency you're counting).

The next few pages will show you lots of examples of each, and give you space to fill in your own igniters and zappers.

Examples of Igniters

SOLITUDE OR QUIET TIME

Moments spent by yourself or in a quiet environment might recharge your energy.

TIME IN NATURE

Nature is especially restorative for Autistic people. If possible, spend time by a lake, near an ocean, or in a meadow, or simply enjoy nature sounds or views of green spaces. Green therapy can greatly rejuvenate your burned-out nervous systems!

SPECIAL INTERESTS

Engaging in hobbies, interests, and pursuits that ignite your passion can provide a significant energy boost.

VITAL BEHAVIORS

Vital behaviors are activities that bring you joy and energize you. These may be related to your special interests or your values. Or they may be related to repetitive physical movements that soothe you (swinging, rhythmic dancing, skating, and so on).

STRUCTURED ROUTINES

Consistency and predictability in daily routines are known to reliably support energy levels.

CREATIVITY

Time spent in creativity can provide a powerful energetic spark while also regrounding you in your authentic self.

PHYSICAL MOVEMENT

Physical movement that brings you joy stimulates the release of endorphins, dopamine, and serotonin. These neurotransmitters play crucial roles in regulating mood, reducing stress, and promoting a sense of well-being—and can provide a powerful energy boost.

DEEP SOCIAL CONNECTION

Strong social connections can energize and spark creativity. These can be in person or online—either way, they should cultivate a sense of belonging.

CALMING SENSORY INPUTS

Specific sensory moments, like the embrace of gentle music or comforting textures, have a way of sparking warmth and vitality within.

MONOTROPIC FLOW

Engaging in tasks that allow for deep, singular focus—a style of concentrated attention natural to many Autistic brains—can be deeply restorative and grounding.

My Igniters

Write down any igniters from the previous page that resonated with you, and add your own ideas as well.

Examples of Zappers

SOCIAL INTERACTIONS AND MASKING

Certain types of social gatherings or prolonged interactions can drain social and sensory energy, more so if you're navigating cross-neurotype interactions.

GOING AGAINST THE GRAIN

Doing things that don't match your natural energy flow can bring on exhaustion more quickly.

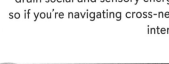

UNTREATED HEALTH CONDITIONS

Conditions that haven't been diagnosed or treated properly can contribute to underlying fatigue.

OVERSTIMULATION

Being in overly stimulating environments can quickly lead to exhaustion.

FOOD ALLERGIES

Eating foods that cause your body to react badly, such as those you are allergic to or ones that cause inflammation can negatively impact your overall health and energy levels.

ROUTINE CHANGES

Unexpected changes or lack of structure in daily routines can lead to energy depletion.

SPECIFIC TASKS OR ACTIVITIES

Certain tasks that require intense focus or are outside your comfort zone may take up more of your energy.

COGNITIVE OVERLOAD

Cognitive overload from activities like decoding complex instructions or navigating too much digital content can quickly lead to mental exhaustion.

EMOTIONAL STRESS

Situations that make you feel upset or anxious can wear you out.

My Zappers

Write down any zappers from the previous page that resonated with you, and add your own ideas as well.

Be Patient with Yourself

As you track your energy, match tasks to your energy levels, and start to discuss your limits with others (see Chapter 8 on self-advocacy), be gentle with yourself. A pacing system should not be a rigid structure that adds to your stress. Instead, it's designed to help you **understand your true capacity, align your actions with your energy levels, and communicate your limits more confidently**. Ideally, it enables you to use your energy more intentionally and mindfully.

Pacing systems also encourage you to make thoughtful choices, recognize your boundaries, and participate in activities that align with your values, guiding your actions to be more intentional and meaningful.

As you explore energy management, **give yourself space to experiment and learn from mistakes**. Finding what works best for you is an essential part of self-care. Here are some other things to keep in mind:

> Some days will be smoother than others.

> The right approaches often involve trial and error.

> What suits you may differ from what works for others.

> Your needs may evolve over time.
> This journey is about continual adaptation and
> learning to respect your changing requirements.

The bottom line: **Energy management is personal and evolving**. The pacing strategies we've discussed in this chapter are tools to help you structure and understand how you use your energy—they are not rigid rules. They're really about cultivating awareness and agency—learning your energy patterns, rhythms, supports, and zappers and then making choices that align your life more closely with your natural energy flow and needs.

CHAPTER 6

Promoting Quality Sleep

The Basics of Sleep

Sleep is a pivotal element in both recovering from burnout and cultivating a life resistant to it. Yet, it's an aspect many Autistic people struggle with! In this chapter, we'll first review why sleep is a challenge for many of us, and then we'll explore the six "sleep buckets" of interventions that can help improve sleep.

Why Sleep Is So Important

Sleep is a vital, yet complex, process that plays a foundational role in maintaining every person's health. **During sleep, your body engages in several important functions**, one of which is the detoxification of your nervous system. This is largely facilitated by the glymphatic system, which actively removes waste products that accumulate during waking hours. Failure to adequately clear out these waste products can result in your waking up feeling groggy and unfocused.

Beyond detoxification, **sleep is essential for a number of functions**. You consolidate learning and memory during sleep—your brain effectively transfers information to long-term memory. Sleep plays an important role for maintaining neurotransmitter balance and regulating mood. It helps ensure that key neurotransmitters like serotonin and dopamine function properly. It's clear that sleep is a critical component of your mental and physical health!

Sleep Disorders in Autistic People

Achieving restful sleep can be particularly challenging for Autistic people due to a myriad of factors. Autism is often linked with various sleep disorders, including:

▶ Sleep-disordered breathing issues, such as sleep apnea

▶ Restless legs syndrome and periodic limb movements

▶ Insomnia, which includes challenges falling asleep and nighttime awakenings

▶ Higher rates of parasomnias, such as sleep terrors, sleep paralysis, and sleepwalking

▶ Delayed sleep-wake phase disorder, which involves having trouble falling asleep and waking up at conventional times

Each of these conditions contributes to the complex picture of Autistic sleep. If you feel you might have any of these, work with your healthcare team to address them.

Autistic Sleep 101

Additional factors affect both sleep quantity and quality in Autistic people. Let's take a look at some of them.

SENSORY SENSITIVITIES

Sensory sensitivities can significantly impact sleep. Sensitivity to environmental stimuli, such as light, not only complicates falling asleep but also disrupts the circadian rhythm by encouraging avoidance of daylight during waking hours.

GENETIC VARIATIONS

Genetic variations common in Autistic people frequently affect melatonin regulation and circadian rhythms. This disruption can lead to a flattened melatonin curve, diminishing the natural sleep signals and complicating the sleep-wake cycle. Co-occurring conditions like anxiety, depression, and gastrointestinal issues further interfere with sleep.

LOWER AMOUNTS OF REM SLEEP

Compounding these challenges, Autistic people often experience less REM sleep—around 15 percent of their sleeping hours compared to the average 20–25 percent. Since REM sleep is essential for restoration, learning, and detoxification, this reduction means that Autistic people require more sleep to feel rested. However, factors such as delayed melatonin secretion and a higher prevalence of breathing-related sleep disorders contribute to poorer sleep quality and efficiency, making sufficient rest elusive for many of us.

ADDRESSING THESE CHALLENGES

Understanding the unique sleep needs and challenges you face is the first step in supporting your sleep. From identifying any potential underlying medical causes to acknowledging the impact of sensory sensitivities to recognizing the intertwined nature of neurodivergent conditions and sleep, this knowledge paves the way for you to curate a tailored sleep plan.

Armed with this information and self-awareness, you can make strides toward improving your sleep by taking steps such as cultivating an environment that accommodates sensory needs and aligns with natural sleep patterns and exploring medical and behavioral interventions for co-occurring conditions.

Recognizing a Poor Sleep Spiral

Many people have experienced poor sleep spirals. These often start with one issue that either pushes your bedtime back dramatically or causes you to lose a lot of sleep one night. The next day, you may need to take unusual steps to manage your energy (such as drinking extra coffee), which then leads to another night of poor sleep. By simply understanding how these cycles of poor sleep take shape, you can take the first step toward better sleep management. Here is a common example of a neurodivergent sleep spiral.

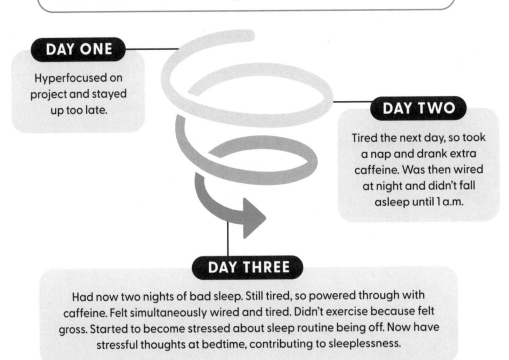

INITIAL SITUATION: Got hyperfocused on a project, stayed up until 2 a.m., but still needed to get up at 6 a.m. for school or work.

DAY ONE

Hyperfocused on project and stayed up too late.

DAY TWO

Tired the next day, so took a nap and drank extra caffeine. Was then wired at night and didn't fall asleep until 1 a.m.

DAY THREE

Had now two nights of bad sleep. Still tired, so powered through with caffeine. Felt simultaneously wired and tired. Didn't exercise because felt gross. Started to become stressed about sleep routine being off. Now have stressful thoughts at bedtime, contributing to sleeplessness.

And so on . . .

The first step to breaking this spiral is becoming aware of the spiral, because once you're aware of your spiral, you can then choose which supports to use to intervene and break the cycle (for example, using cognitive strategies to disrupt stressful sleep thoughts or shifting your routine). Things that help break the cycle are your "sleep resets," and you'll find several suggestions throughout this chapter.

Identify Your Sleep Stressors and Agitators

Sleep is a delicate thing, particularly for Autistic people. We've got a lot working against us, and one simple thing can throw off our sleep cycle for days! Knowing your sleep agitators is helpful. These are the environmental, situational, social, and mood agitators that disrupt your sleep. Jotting down notes on your stressors will help you identify which parts of your sleep need the most support. Use the space here to record the agitators that are relevant to you. The examples in parentheses are examples to get you thinking, but be sure to consider your personal stressors, as they will differ for each individual.

SITUATIONAL AGITATORS	ENVIRONMENTAL AGITATORS	SOCIAL AGITATORS
(Sickness, disruption to routine, working late, etc.)	*(Sounds, smells, textures, etc.)*	*(Partner sleep habits, social events, etc.)*

MOOD AGITATORS	PHYSICAL AGITATORS	DIETARY AGITATORS
(Anxiety, stress, depression, etc.)	*(Pain, physical restlessness, GI discomfort, etc.)*	*(Caffeine, sugar, alcohol, late meals, etc.)*

SLEEP SPIRAL HABITS

Lastly, pinpoint any recurring poor sleep spirals, such as staying up late, then compensating with naps and caffeine the following day, that you have experienced.

Identify Your Sleep Resets

If your sleep agitators are the things that send you into a poor sleep spiral, sleep resets are the things that help you get back on track. For example:

▶ Successfully pushing through a day without a nap or extra caffeine to help you return to your normal sleep time.

▶ Using a sleep aid (over-the-counter or prescribed) to get back onto a regular schedule.

▶ Engaging in exercise during the day so that you're more sleepy at night and can return to your typical sleep rhythm.

Take a moment to consider and write down the practices that help you reset your sleep cycle when it has gotten off track. If you don't have any yet, that is okay. After you've worked through this chapter, come back and see if you can use some of the strategies from this chapter as sleep resets.

Building a
SLEEP SUPPORT SYSTEM

Just as everyone needs a social support system, you might benefit from a sleep support system as well. Some of the common themes for sleep supports involve:

- **CREATING A FAVORABLE SLEEP ENVIRONMENT:** Tailoring your space to meet your sensory needs and practicing good sleep hygiene can have a beneficial impact on your sleep. Plus, creating a strong "bed = sleep" connection can prepare your body for sleep.

- **TACTICS FOR PUTTING A BUSY MIND TO SLEEP:** If your active neurodivergent mind is keeping you up, spend time on the CBT-I (cognitive behavioral therapy for insomnia) section of this chapter.

- **WAYS TO SOOTHE A HYPERACTIVE NERVOUS SYSTEM:** For a hyperactive nervous system that just can't settle, it can be helpful to start with relaxation exercises.

This chapter presents a variety of strategies because there's no one-size-fits-all solution to sleep challenges. I encourage you to select and focus on practices that best match your specific needs. Due to the wide range of sleep issues and their causes, I find it helpful to organize the topics into different "buckets of support" when helping people with their sleep. These are the six primary buckets I typically draw from and find helpful when working with sleep issues:

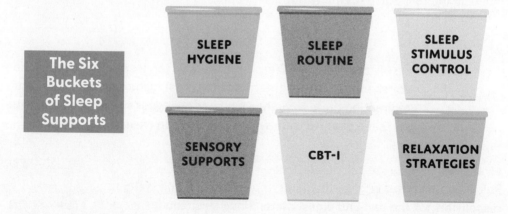

The Six Buckets of Sleep Supports

SLEEP HYGIENE

SLEEP ROUTINE

SLEEP STIMULUS CONTROL

SENSORY SUPPORTS

CBT-I

RELAXATION STRATEGIES

You'll find an overview about these buckets on the next page, then an in-depth look at each bucket after that.

The Six Buckets of Sleep Support

SLEEP HYGIENE

"Sleep hygiene" simply refers to habits that help you get a good night's sleep. Just as dental and bodily hygiene keep you healthy, sleep hygiene helps prepare your body for healthy sleep.

A consistent sleep routine signals to your brain and body that it's time to rest. The more regularly you follow your routine, the stronger the link between the routine and sleep. Additionally, maintaining consistent sleep and wake times reinforces your circadian rhythm.

SLEEP ROUTINE

SLEEP STIMULUS CONTROL

Your brain quickly forms associations, including between various stimuli (like sounds, smells, and places) and sleep. Sleep stimulus control focuses on safeguarding your sleep environment to ensure it's associated solely with sleep.

Sensitivities to temperature, fabric, light, and sounds can all interfere with sleep. Cultivating the ideal sensory sleep experience can help improve sleep for many Autistic people.

SENSORY SUPPORTS

CBT-I

CBT-I, or cognitive behavioral therapy for insomnia, targets the stress-inducing thoughts that often fuel insomnia. By altering or redirecting these thoughts, which trigger your stress response, you can calm your nervous system, facilitating easier sleep onset.

Relaxation exercises engage the parasympathetic nervous system, responsible for the rest-and-digest state. Since sleep eludes us in the alertness-driven sympathetic mode, these exercises are crucial for transitioning to the relaxed state your body needs for sleep.

RELAXATION STRATEGIES

More on Sleep Hygiene

What Is Sleep Hygiene?

Sleep hygiene involves habits that enhance your sleep quality. Key practices include sleeping in a dark, cool environment and reserving the bed exclusively for sleep (and intimacy). These habits foster a healthy connection between the bedroom and restful sleep.

Why Is Sleep Hygiene Important?

Sleep hygiene is important for everyone, but even more so for the Autistic person. Many of us struggle to maintain healthy rhythms and routines and are prone to unhealthy sleep-wake patterns and cycles. We also have additional genetic vulnerabilities predisposing us to poor sleep, so we benefit from being extra vigilant about sleep hygiene to offset these vulnerabilities. Sleep hygiene tasks are also more difficult for us to complete, so it's important to be gentle and kind with yourself as you work to implement these practices.

Here are some beneficial sleep hygiene strategies. You'll take an inventory of your current sleep hygiene habits on the next page.

SLEEP HYGIENE PRACTICES

Have a sleep routine.

Sleep in a cold, dark, and quiet room.

Get up and go to sleep at consistent times.

Avoid caffeine and naps after 2 p.m.

Turn screens off early and find a tech-free way to unwind.

Move your body regularly. (But avoid vigorous exercise within two hours of bedtime.)

Avoid alcohol and heavy meals two hours prior to bed.

Assess Your Sleep Hygiene Practices

Review this list. Check the boxes you've got covered, and circle the areas to work on.

- ○ *I go to bed and wake up at the same time every day.*
- ○ *I avoid caffeine and naps after 2 p.m.*
- ○ *I sleep in a cold room.*
- ○ *I turn screens off early and find a tech-free way to unwind.*
- ○ *I avoid alcohol and heavy meals two hours prior to bed.*
- ○ *I sleep in a dark room (or use a sleep mask).*
- ○ *I sleep in a quiet room (or use a white noise machine).*
- ○ *I have a consistent sleep routine.*
- ○ *I move my body regularly but avoid vigorous exercise two hours before bedtime.*

ONE SLEEP HYGIENE GOAL

Look over the information you discovered in the checklist, and write one simple goal you can try to achieve to improve your sleep hygiene.

More on Sleep Routine

What Is a Sleep Routine?

A sleep routine primes the brain and body, cuing that it is time to sleep. Our brains and bodies rely on both internal cues (like hormonal changes) and external cues to signal sleep readiness. For Autistic people, who often experience a less pronounced melatonin curve, establishing a sleep routine becomes crucial.

Why Is a Sleep Routine Important?

A consistent sleep routine sends signals to your brain that it is time to unwind and relax. Calming rituals prepare the body and mind for sleep. Over time, these serve as consistent external signals to prepare for rest, helping to compensate for the more subdued internal cues that many of us experience.

Additionally, having a consistent wake routine and bedtime routine helps to synchronize your sleep-wake cycle and strengthens your circadian rhythm—a common challenge among Autistic people—thereby improving overall sleep quality. One quick tip: Consistency is key! A three-minute bedtime routine done consistently is more beneficial than a fifteen-minute routine practiced sporadically.

RELAXING SLEEP ROUTINE IDEAS

Read a book.

Take a warm bath or shower.

Have a self-care routine you love.

Drink herbal tea.

Use your favorite essential oil (your brain will begin to pair this with sleep).

Do some gentle stretches or yoga.

Engage in relaxation exercises.

Spend five minutes gratitude journaling.

Assess Your Sleep Routine

Do you have a consistent sleep and wake time each day?

○ **YES**   ○ **NO**   ○ **KIND OF**   *How much time do you typically need to unwind?*

List any practices or activities you consistently do before bed (lock door, change clothes, wash face, brush teeth, read, stretch, etc.).

List any activities you experience as relaxing or that help you unwind (bath, reading, solitaire, etc.).

What parts of your nightly routine interfere with your sleep or act as a trigger for poor sleep?

What parts of your nightly routine support your sleep and/or function as sleep resets?

If you were to create one sleep routine goal based on what you've learned, what would it be?

⊚ **ONE SLEEP ROUTINE GOAL**

Create Your Ideal Sleep Routine

Thirty minutes before bed

✓ *Read a book*

Getting ready for bed

✓ *Change*
✓ *Do gentle stretches*
✓ *Wash face*
✓ *Brush teeth*

In bed

✓ *Put eye mask on*
✓ *Practice progressive muscle relaxation*
✓ *Reflect on what I'm grateful for*

My Ideal Sleep Routine

Thirty minutes before bed

Getting ready for bed

In bed

List any potential blocks or barriers that interfere with your sleep routine.

More on Sleep Stimulus Control

What Is Sleep Stimulus Control?

Sleep stimulus control is the process of connecting certain items or practices with sleep. You'll do this by training your brain to connect the two things (for example, when you climb into bed, your brain will know it's time to sleep) using neuroplasticity. Neuroplasticity, simply put, is your brain's ability to adapt to new situations by forming new neural pathways. This principle is crucial when you aim to transform your sleep patterns.

Why Is Sleep Stimulus Control Important?

These neural pathways are important because they are the means by which associations form. Donald Hebb, a renowned neuropsychologist, captured this idea with the phrase "Neurons that fire together, wire together." Hebb was describing the concept of neural associations. Consider how you form habits in your daily life as an example of this process. Imagine that you eat chips when you watch TV every Friday night for months and months. Over time, your brain begins to link these two activities, creating a new neural pathway.

When neurons become associated, one cue—like turning on the TV—automatically triggers a craving for its pair, such as chips. Thus, simply sitting down to watch TV may spark a desire for chips because your brain has linked them together. Each time this pathway is activated (and you eat chips while watching TV), this pathway strengthens.

This concept extends to environments too. If you always work in a specific area, you condition your brain to associate that space with work. Similarly, sleeping soundly in one part of your house teaches your brain to associate that area with rest. However, if you spend nights tossing, turning, and stressing in your bed, your brain will link your bed with stress—a catastrophic association for sleep health! Unfortunately, this is a common trap many of us fall into.

The Connection Between Insomnia and Poor Sleep Stimulus Control

Neural Associations and Insomnia

The brain's tendency to form neural connections is part of why people get stuck in insomnia loops. If you struggle with insomnia, your brain begins to associate sleep, bed, and nighttime with stress, which then perpetuates the insomnia cycle. When it comes to sleep, you want to have a very strong "bed equals sleep" association. However, many of us have a disrupted association between bed and sleep.

Several things can interfere with the association between bed and sleep. Two of the most common are:

1 *Doing activities other than sleep (or intimacy) in your bed.*

2 *Having negative associations with the bed (commonly seen in the context of insomnia, where you toss and turn). Additionally, people with complex health conditions, who may spend extended periods in bed due to illness or pain, might also develop negative associations with their beds. This, in turn, can further complicate sleep, adding another layer to the challenge of cultivating a positive bed-sleep relationship.*

Why It's Difficult to Create New Neural Pathways

When I was younger, I used to do a lot of backpacking, and sometimes we had to navigate off the traditional trails and "bushwhack," or carve out new paths, to get to our destination. These unofficial trails were barely noticeable at first, but with repeated use, they became well-defined and easier to navigate. This process mirrors how your brain adapts to new experiences. Initially, a new neural pathway is like a barely visible trail and is challenging to navigate, but with each repeated experience, this path becomes more pronounced, solidified, and easier to traverse.

This process explains why it's easier to break habits or addiction when a person changes their environment—the new setting lacks the established associations that trigger old behaviors. Similarly, this is why sleeping can become difficult in a room associated with work or stress—your brain has linked the environment with alertness, not rest, making the path to sleep more challenging. Many Autistic people have years of stressed relationships to sleep! So, these pathways in your brain could be deeply engraved. This means it takes a bit of effort (and patience) to create new associations and neural pathways.

Assess Your Sleep Stimulus Control

Fortunately, the concept of neuroplasticity offers a means for breaking this cycle. By establishing a consistent bedtime routine and practicing good sleep hygiene, you can teach your brain to forge more helpful associations. Sleep stimulus is one way you can cultivate positive associations and reduce the negative ones.

Review this list. Check the boxes you've got covered and circle the areas to work on.

- **AVOID WATCHING THE CLOCK:** *Checking the time can keep you alert. Try turning the clock away from your view.*
- **TURN OFF YOUR PHONE:** *Using your phone in bed leads your brain to associate the bed with wakefulness.*
- **SLEEP EXCLUSIVELY IN YOUR BEDROOM:** *Avoid dozing off in other places, like in a recliner, which can weaken the association between your bed and sleep.*
- **RESERVE YOUR BEDROOM FOR SLEEP (AND INTIMACY):** *This strengthens the mental link between your bedroom and rest.*
- **WAIT TO BE SLEEPY BEFORE GOING TO BED:** *This ensures that your bed is associated with the act of falling asleep, not just lying awake.*
- **HAVE A STRONG BEDTIME ROUTINE:** *Engaging in a nightly routine signals to your body that it's time to wind down.*
- **USE RELAXATION STRATEGIES:** *Associating your bed with relaxation techniques teaches the brain to link relaxation with bedtime, counteracting stress.*
- **IMPLEMENT SENSORY CUES:** *Using a specific essential oil or other sensory cue only at night can train the brain to associate it with sleep readiness.*

If you were to create one sleep stimulus control goal based on what you've learned, what would it be?

ONE SLEEP STIMULUS CONTROL GOAL

How to Create Positive Associations with Bed

The initial phase of sleep stimulus control is all about cutting down on anything that messes with the straightforward "bed = sleep" connection. Following that, it's key to tackle any negative feelings you've built up around your bed and start replacing them with positive associations. This can feel like a bit of a hurdle, especially if your ongoing battles with sleep have left you with a bit of a love-hate relationship with your sleeping space. Here are some actions you can take to break the cycle and replace those negative associations with more positive ones.

1 Implement the Fifteen-Minute Rule

One effective strategy is to limit the amount of time you spend *awake* in bed. Here's how it works: If you find yourself awake and restless after fifteen minutes, leave the bed and engage in a calming activity, like doing a crossword, reading, or stretching gently. Return to bed only when you feel sleepy. This approach minimizes stress-related time in bed, gradually reshaping your brain's association from "bed = stress" to "bed = sleep." Use the space here to jot down calming activities you could try if you need to leave your bed after fifteen minutes.

2 Create a Favorable Sleep Environment

Creating a sleep environment that is delightful to your senses (we'll explore this in more detail in the sensory supports bucket) can also help build positive associations. For example:

> **Practice relaxation techniques as you drift to sleep.**

> **Establish a sensory-pleasing bedroom experience.**

Now write down any positive associations you currently have with your bed that you could build on.

③ Set Up Another Part of Your Bedroom for Nonsleep Activities

Navigating sleep stimulus control can be especially tricky for Autistic people. Our bedrooms, and very often our beds, become our sanctuaries for alone time. But as tempting as it is to camp out in bed all day, it's not the best for our sleep health. It might not be realistic to turn your whole bedroom into a sleep-only zone, but there's a middle ground: You could set up a comfy nook with a chair or desk in your room for everything else, like chilling, working, scrolling, or diving into a good book. This way, you're sending your brain a clear message: Bed is for sleeping, not for hangouts or work marathons.

Brainstorm on the lines here any minor changes you could make to your bedroom to keep your bed focused on sleep.

What Are Sensory Supports?

Sensory supports are items or practices that help you manage any sensory sensitivities you have that are associated with sleep. Sensory sensitivities can wreak havoc on your sleep! Ideal temperatures and textures help everyone sleep better, but they are even more important to the hypersensitive person.

Why Are Sensory Supports Important?

Sensitivities to temperature shifts, fabric discomfort, light, and sounds can all interfere with sleep. Cultivating the ideal sensory-sleep experience can help improve sleep for many Autistic people. (Bonus: This will also help create positive associations with bed!)

It's important not to look down on sensory supports. Sometimes I think of accommodations as my "second skin." My "skin" (my sensory profile) so often fails to create a barrier between myself and the world, and then the world easily overwhelms me. So, I patch together a "second skin" to provide a barrier.

"Accommodations" sounds like a fancy word. But in reality, accommodations are anything that helps you adapt your environment to better fit your needs. We'll talk more about them on the next page.

Assess Your Sensory Supports

In the same way that many Autistic people benefit from work, school, and household accommodations, we also benefit from sleep accommodations. Until I thought of these things as accommodations, I thought about them in a more negative light, like "being a fussy sleeper" or "being high-maintenance." Or I simply refused to invest in a quality mattress or sleep gear as I considered them to be overly indulgent. Once I realized these were accommodations that helped me function better in the world, it gave me permission to invest in my sleep.

Here are a few common sleep accommodations. Check off any that might work for you, and add your own ideas in the blank spaces provided.

- *A quality eye mask to block out light*
- *Blackout curtains*
- *A sound machine*
- *Earplugs*
- *A memory foam mattress and pillow for comfort (or your sensory system may prefer an ultrafirm mattress!)*
- *A weighted blanket*
- *Sleeping alone instead of with a partner*
- *Wearing either loose or constricting pajamas based on your preferences*
- *Using essential oils or applying a scented lotion*
- *A fan to encourage airflow*

If you were to create one sensory support goal based on what you've learned, what would it be?

ONE SENSORY SUPPORT GOAL

More on CBT-I
(Cognitive Behavioral Therapy for Insomnia)

What Is CBT-I?

Many of us wrestle with busy minds, especially at night, making sleep elusive. Thus, techniques to help quiet your thoughts are incredibly useful. Although I'm typically cautious about suggesting cognitive behavioral therapy for Autistic people, CBT-I stands out as an exception. This specific approach targets the stressful thought patterns surrounding sleep. These worries perpetuate the cycle of insomnia by triggering your stress response, leading to a tense relationship with sleep marked by negative beliefs and fears.

Why Is CBT-I Important?

Common worries like "I'll never fall asleep" or "Tomorrow will be terrible" amplify stress, engaging your body's alert system. That alert system triggers a surge of cortisol and adrenaline, further waking you! If you're struggling with sleep night after night, it is very understandable to have catastrophic thoughts associated with sleep. While these thoughts are justified, they simply aren't helpful, and they're actually making sleep more difficult for you. For this reason, I find it helpful to shift thoughts into something more gentle and reassuring, as it helps us get out of our stress response!

Shifting worrisome thoughts to more soothing ones, like "I've managed before; I can do so tonight," helps signal safety to your nervous system, increasing your chances of drifting off to sleep. An important note: You can shift thoughts while still validating that it's a hard and painful moment.

Understanding and Interrupting the Negative Sleep Talk Spiral

This diagram gives you a visual of how stressful thoughts about sleep perpetuate the insomnia loop and identifies spots where you can intervene.

START

1 You are lying in bed, unable fall asleep.

2 Stress thoughts about sleep, such as "I will never get to sleep," "I am going to feel so miserable tomorrow," etc., arrive.

3 Stress thoughts activate a stress response in your body (sympathetic mode). Your body is filled with cortisol and adrenaline. It is now harder to fall asleep.

4 You're tossing and turning in bed in a stressed state. Now the bed is associated with stress. This fuels more negative thoughts about sleep.

5 The cycle is off and running.

REPEAT

INTERVENING WITH THE CYCLE

We can intervene with this sleep spiral at Step 2 by addressing stress thoughts. You can disrupt the cycle with either self-soothing statements (see the next page) or with mental distraction techniques (see the exercise Practice Cognitive Shuffling in this chapter).

Crafting Self-Soothing Statements

You can intervene and disrupt a negative sleep cycle with something called cognitive reframing. Instead of engaging the stress thoughts, you can create more gentle, self-soothing thoughts.

NEGATIVE THOUGHT		SELF-SOOTHING STATEMENT	EXPLANATION OF THE COGNITIVE REFRAMING
I will never fall asleep.	➡	I will eventually fall asleep.	Reduces catastrophic and fear-based thinking, provides self-reassurance.
I am going to feel miserable tomorrow.	➡	I have survived tired days before.	Shifts from disempowering, agitated tone to resilience mindset.
I am so frustrated I can't fall asleep.	➡	This is a hard moment—this is painful.	Shifts energy from agitation toward self-attunement and self-compassion.

 Now it is your turn. First, identify some of your common "stress sleep thoughts," then see if you can come up with an alternative thought that still feels honest and provides a compassionate or self-soothing alternative.

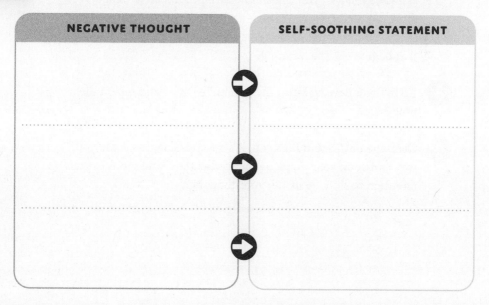

NEGATIVE THOUGHT		SELF-SOOTHING STATEMENT
	➡	
	➡	
	➡	

Practice Cognitive Shuffling

Cognitive shuffling involves intentionally mixing up your thoughts until they lose their logical sequence. This mental activity eases your mind from alertness into sleepiness. It also interrupts the mind's tendency to evaluate, plan, and ruminate—processes that often keep us awake. For a guided experience of this technique, check out the MySleepButton app, which offers a practical application of cognitive shuffling to help induce sleep. To try it yourself, follow these instructions.

Self-Directed Cognitive Shuffling

Here's how to direct yourself through a cognitive shuffling exercise:

1 Pick any word. Let's use "garden."

2 Think of a word that starts with the first letter of that word (in this case, "g"). For example, "garbage." Now bring up the mental image of garbage or a garbage can. (If you have aphantasia or can't see images, you can simply bring the word to mind.) Now think of another word that begins with the letter "g" and bring to mind that mental image. Keep going until you run out of words that begin with the letter "g."

3 Go to the following letter in "garden"—"a"—and repeat the process.

4 Continue until you fall asleep. If stressful thoughts come your way and hook your mind, acknowledge them and redirect your attention back to shuffling your thoughts.

Create a Worry Period

So far, we've explored several methods for managing a busy mind. Another helpful practice, one you can incorporate during the day (just be careful not to do this too close to bedtime), is creating a "worry period." The mind often craves attention, which is why, when you try to fall asleep, worry thoughts tend to surface with full force.

Worry itself isn't inherently bad—it often gets a bad reputation. In reality, worry is how we solve problems and come up with solutions. **The goal is not to eliminate worry but to learn how to worry well.** One way to do this is to designate a specific period of fifteen to twenty minutes during which your sole focus is to worry mindfully and productively.

How to Utilize a Worry Period

1 **SET UP YOUR PAGE:** Grab a piece of paper and draw two columns. Label the columns "In My Control" and "Out of My Control" (you can also add a third, "Not Sure"). (See the next page for an example.)

2 **WORRY DUMP:** Think of all the worries currently swirling in your mind and write them down in the appropriate columns.

3 **MAKE AN ACTION PLAN:** For worries in your control, pick one or two and create an action plan. What is one step you can take to address each concern?

4 **PRACTICE RELEASING:** For worries outside your control, focus on releasing them. You can do this through spiritual practice if it aligns with you, or by practicing mindful detachment, reminding yourself these worries are beyond your influence.

What Are Your Worries?

This template can help you organize and release your worries during your worry period. During other times (especially at night), if a worry pops into your head, gently acknowledge it and remind yourself that you'll address it during your designated worry period. This process helps create a mental container for your worries—you reassure your mind that these concerns will be handled at the appropriate time. You then free yourself to redirect your attention and release that worry—and hopefully sleep better.

IN MY CONTROL	OUT OF MY CONTROL	NOT SURE

Make a Plan for Your Worries

One action I can take to address a worry on my list that is in my control:

One practice that helps me release a worry that is out of my control:

More on Relaxation Strategies

What Are Relaxation Strategies and Why Are They Important?

Relaxation strategies are tools that help to get the body out of the sympathetic mode (stress state), which is essential for initiating sleep. Incorporating relaxation strategies into your bedtime routine can be so helpful because they tie together many of the themes we've already talked about—calming your body and mind, creating positive associations with your bed, and building a strong bedtime routine.

Examples of Relaxation Strategies

Here are some exercises that you could consider including in your nighttime routine. Check off any ideas that seem like they might work for you, and choose one to try. You can also add your own techniques in the blank spaces.

- **INTENTIONAL SLOW, DEEP BREATHING:** *Focus on taking slow, deep breaths to calm the mind and body.*
- **PROGRESSIVE MUSCLE RELAXATION:** *Tense and then relax each muscle group in sequence to release physical stress.*
- **VISUALIZATIONS:** *Immerse yourself in peaceful scenes or stories.*
- **GUIDED MEDITATIONS AND RELAXATION APPS:** *Use apps like Calm, which offer guided meditations and meditative scripts specifically designed for sleep.*
- **GENTLE YOGA:** *Incorporate calming poses, such as Child's Pose, which can help promote relaxation. Be mindful that some yoga positions can be more activating, so focus on those that encourage rest and calm.*
- **NATURE SOUNDS OR MEDITATIVE SCRIPTS:** *Similar to guided meditations, these sounds are crafted to facilitate sleep onset.*
- **VAGAL NERVE STIMULATORS:** *Devices like the Sensate or a TENS unit with ear clips can help calm the nervous system.*

After you try the idea you selected, reflect in the space here on how it worked for you. What did you observe about your physical and mental state before and after the exercise? Would you try it again? Is there anything you would change about how you did it?

Benefits of Quality Sleep

The Autistic sleep experience is undoubtedly one of the things that predisposes us to burnout. Lack of adequate sleep wears on our nervous system and physical health, making us more prone to burnout. Implementing small, supportive changes to your sleep habits can, over time, have a big impact. When you improve your sleep quality (or quantity), you might find that you've:

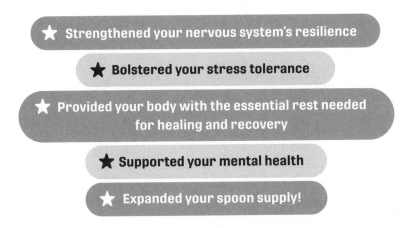

★ Strengthened your nervous system's resilience

★ Bolstered your stress tolerance

★ Provided your body with the essential rest needed for healing and recovery

★ Supported your mental health

★ Expanded your spoon supply!

When I worked in a hospital with complex medical and mental health cases, I often found that the most impactful place to start was with improving sleep. The difference between getting just one full sleep cycle and missing out on sleep can be the tipping point between balance and a breakdown. At the risk of being dramatic, I can't overemphasize the critical role sleep plays in your mental and physical well-being.

That being said, there's no need to adopt every strategy in this chapter simultaneously. Instead, I recommend selecting the practices that most directly address your current sleep challenges, crafting a tailored approach.

CHAPTER 7

Understanding Masking and Burnout

The Double-Edged Sword of Masking

This chapter focuses on reducing stress by cutting down on masking. We'll briefly define masking, examine its connection to burnout, and discuss ways to unmask or at least become more intentional in our use of masking.

The tough thing about masking is that it's a double-edged sword because **masking isn't entirely good or bad**. For example, my ability to mask grants me advantages, helps me navigate systems like education and healthcare, and has helped me secure jobs. In social situations where being perceived as different might cause stress or danger, I can suppress Autistic traits. **There is privilege that comes with my ability to mask.**

On the other hand, masking is detrimental to mental health and energy and is thought to contribute to burnout, substance abuse, and suicidality. Even though it can have benefits in some areas, **it's important to acknowledge that masking isn't good for your well-being**. But living in a world where you face discrimination, isolation, and misunderstanding is also harmful to your mental health and self-esteem. Sometimes, masking is portrayed as a terrible thing—as if unmasking would solve all your problems—but that's not true either. The reality is, neither option is ideal.

Ideally, we would live in a neuro-inclusive world that embraced all bodies and their regulation needs, like stimming, and all forms of communication. However, we don't yet live in that world, leaving us with the double-edged sword of masking. Additionally, some Autistic people wish they could mask but aren't able to, and they are often left out of the unmasking conversation. Others are so used to masking that they long to know who they are beneath the mask. My hope is that, as a community, **we can have compassion for the complexity of experiences surrounding masking and unmasking**.

Masking, Defined

Au·tis·tic mask·ing (compound noun)

Autistic masking involves the conscious or unconscious efforts of an Autistic person to change their external behavior and hide aspects of themselves to avoid harm, using strategies such as:

- Suppressing stimming behaviors
- Meticulously studying and imitating social behaviors
- Analyzing body language
- Scripting and rehearsing conversations
- Exhibiting excessive accommodation and helpfulness toward others

Also referred to as "camouflaging," masking is essentially how we adapt to our environment. Dr. Laura Hull, a research fellow at Bristol Medical School, found three distinct ways that people camouflage their autism: compensation, masking, and assimilation:

COMPENSATION: *Mimicking and copying allistic (non-Autistic) people*

MASKING: *Actively suppressing Autistic traits*

ASSIMILATION: *Engaging in behaviors that don't come naturally and often cause significant discomfort*

You can take a test called the CAT-Q that determines how deeply you are masking (Embrace Autism has it available for free on their website).

Why Do Autistic People Mask?

Early research focused on masking being an adaptive strategy used so that a person could fit in socially. More recent research in 2021—led by Autistic researchers Dr. Amy Pearson and Kieran Rose—highlighted how masking is a much more complex—and often unconscious—drive for safety that developed as a trauma response.

MASKING = An Instinctual Drive for Safety

This categorization of Autistic camouflaging comes from the work of Laura Hull et al., "Development and Validation of the Camouflaging Autistic Traits Questionnaire (CAT-Q)," published in 2019. Research by Amy Pearson and Kieran Rose, "A Conceptual Analysis of Autistic Masking: Understanding the Narrative of Stigma and the Illusion of Choice," focuses on masking as an innate drive for safety.

Mimicking Others' Behavior

Autistic people who mask often possess an exceptional ability to observe, analyze, and dissect allistic social cues. Many of us develop a heightened vigilance regarding the people around us in order to adapt, much like chameleons adapting to their environments. We meticulously study how people move, talk, and interact. A lot of us take on this role of social detective and social scientist from an early age.

I often talk about my "social research" as though I were using a mental Google Doc. Every time I saw someone navigate social situations in a way I liked, I'd mentally jot it down. I might note, "I like how they move their hand" or "I like that phrase." Then I'd mimic those behaviors. Over the years, I collected a whole repertoire of actions and phrases from different people.

Does this habit of collecting information about social situations resonate with you? Write down your thoughts about that topic here.

How Autistic Masking Affects Identity

Masking Becomes Part of Your Core Identity

Masking becomes so interwoven with our psyches that it's hard to distinguish the threads of our authentic selves from the threads of our masked personas.

Masking often develops at a young age, and many people are not even aware they are masking! Many Autistic children receive feedback on their behavior that leads them to mask. For example, when a child faces harsh discipline for their Autistic traits like stimming, asking questions, avoiding eye contact, or experiencing sensory meltdowns, they may respond by learning to mask these traits as a survival mechanism. Striving to please others and evade punishment becomes their natural way of navigating the world, deeply ingrained and often unconscious, intertwining with their core identity during their formative years.

Do you notice yourself engaging in any behaviors that may have developed as a survival mechanism? Reflect on them here.

Unmasking to Truly Understand Yourself

Because masking is likely embedded in your psyche, "unmasking" is much more complex than simply taking off the mask to find your "true self." Your true self and the mask are often interwoven in complex ways. You don't simply start stimming, stop making eye contact, and quit small talk to suddenly find yourself. I wish it were that easy!

Unmasking is about deeply understanding yourself, not just swapping out behaviors (like making eye contact) for others (avoiding eye contact). **Focusing solely on external forms of unmasking misses the important aspects of understanding who you are: your pleasures, delights, preferences, soothers, passions, and more.**

Masking and Intersecting Identities

Interest in Autistic masking largely began with investigating why many Autistic girls and women go undiagnosed. Researchers realized that girls and women were more likely to mask, which delayed their diagnosis or meant it was missed altogether. Early research, however, overlooked the genderqueer population, perpetuating a binary view of gender. Over time, research has expanded to consider how masking affects all individuals.

Anyone Can Mask

Autistic masking knows no bounds—**anyone can mask, regardless of age, gender, or background**. It is especially common among Autistic people with average to above-average intelligence and is prevalent among girls, women, BIPOC, and genderqueer individuals. However, many cis-het white men also mask.

Similar to code-switching, where individuals from nonwhite cultures adjust their speech and behavior to fit into white-dominant spaces, masking involves adapting to neuro-normative behaviors and communication styles. **Autistic people of color, who may be both code-switching and masking, experience compounded exhaustion.**

Understanding Intersectionality

The experience of masking intersects with gender, race, and identity in complex ways. **"Intersectionality" refers to how multiple forms of discrimination— such as discrimination due to race, gender, and disability—interact to create unique, cumulative effects.** For example, an Autistic Black woman faces challenges that aren't just a sum of being Black, female, or Autistic. She experiences racism differently from Black men and sexism differently from white women, and her autism might be misunderstood or neglected due to racial and gender biases. These intersecting identities compound and intensify the discrimination and barriers she faces, creating a distinct experience that can't be fully understood by looking at each identity in isolation.

Remember, Masking Provides Safety

We cannot advocate for all Autistic people to unmask until it is safe to be Black, Brown, Queer, and trans. Masking is a safety strategy, and **those with multiple marginalized identities need its protection more than others**. This is why masking should be approached from a harm-reduction standpoint rather than as something to be eliminated.

The term and concept of intersectionality was introduced in an essay by **Kimberlé Crenshaw**, "Demarginalizing the Intersection of Race and Sex: A Black Feminist Critique of Antidiscrimination Doctrine, Feminist Theory and Antiracist Politics," *U. Chi. Legal* (1989): 139–67.

Ways That Masking
CONTRIBUTES TO BURNOUT

While Autistic masking comes with some advantages, such as the ability to pass as allistic and navigate workplaces and educational settings with less stigma, it also comes with significant costs. Most notably, it is one of the main contributors to burnout, depression, substance abuse, and more. Autistic people with fewer traditional support needs (such as support navigating daily tasks) often have very high mental health support needs (such as managing anxiety and depression), and one of the reasons for this is masking.

There are many factors that contribute to the masking-burnout link. For example, if you're masking, you're more likely to be undiagnosed or misdiagnosed (which contributes to burnout), and you also lack access to stimming and self-soothing behaviors (which also contributes to burnout). The factors shown on this page can all worsen burnout.

OVERRIDING YOUR NATURAL INSTINCTS TO SELF-SOOTHE and regulate your body

DISCONNECTION FROM SELF, which makes it harder to identify and respond to internal stressors

UNDERSTANDING THE
MASKING-BURNOUT LINK

Experiencing **THE "MASKING PARADOX,"** in which masking not only heightens stress but also makes it harder to access support and accommodations

The **FAWN RESPONSE AND PEOPLE-PLEASING,** which often lead you to override your own needs in order to satisfy others

Putting extra **STRAIN ON THE PREFRONTAL CORTEX**

The next several pages will go into each of these topics in more depth and give you journaling space to reflect on any experiences you have with them.

DISCONNECTION FROM SELF

One way masking contributes to burnout is that it makes it harder to connect with yourself and your body's signals. Being in tune with your inner state is key for self-care. When you mask, a significant amount of energy is devoted to interpreting and responding to others' cues. It's as if you've developed a hypersensitive antenna for picking up signals from those around you. This constant vigilance can disconnect you from your internal signals, needs, and experiences. This disconnection hinders your ability to self-regulate and makes you more vulnerable to developing mood disorders like depression, anxiety, and even PTSD.

For many of us, surviving in this world has involved avoiding our own bodily needs and desires. Consequently, identifying mounting stress and responding to it proves challenging. Through masking, we override our signals, leading to a cycle that often culminates in extreme burnout or a mental health crisis. By the time intervention happens, we are often in crisis mode, making recovery much harder.

Recovering from burnout and managing your mental health require being in touch with your body, recognizing your needs, and responding with care. We'll talk about this more on the next page.

In the space here, consider reflecting on how strongly you feel connected to your inner self. Are there times you are better able to assess your needs than others? What times are particularly challenging?

Interoceptive Awareness Builders

Dr. Kelly Mahler, a sensory-based occupational therapist, has significantly contributed to our understanding of **interoception**—the perception of internal body signals—and its importance in emotion regulation and self-regulation. (Interoceptive awareness is the ability to perceive, identify, and understand internal signals such as the urge to urinate or eliminate, fullness, hunger, cramps, thirst, pain, tension, emotions, and your heartbeat.) Mahler coined the term **"IA Builders"** (Interoceptive Awareness Builders) to describe exercises and strategies designed to improve interoceptive awareness. While working with a sensory-based OT can be helpful, there are also exercises you can do on your own. Check any that might work for you.

○ **CREATE A SENSATION AND NOTICE IT.** *Intentionally bring your attention to a sensation. For example, hold a warm or cold beverage and focus on how it feels in your hands. Adding these mindful moments throughout the day can improve interoceptive awareness. Alternatively, try stretching and bring your attention to the sensations in your muscles.*

○ **FOCUS ON YOUR HEARTBEAT AND TRY TO NOTICE IT.** *Sit quietly and try to feel your heart beating without touching your body. You can also use a wearable tracker with haptic feedback, which vibrates in sync with your pulse to enhance awareness. Biofeedback or heart rate–tracking games that monitor your pulse and encourage mindful breathing are other options.*

○ **DO A BODY SCAN.** *Set aside a few minutes to focus on different parts of your body, moving from head to toe. Pay attention to the physical sensations in each area—whether it's tension, warmth, tingling, or any other feeling. The key is to notice these sensations without judgment.*

Incorporating these moments throughout your day can gradually improve interoceptive awareness.

FAWN RESPONSE AND PEOPLE-PLEASING

Masking often results in a tendency to default into a fawn response or people-pleasing mode. The fawn response is a stress response where we prioritize pleasing others to maintain harmony. Many Autistic people who mask have learned to blend in by taking up less space and being helpful to those around them. This people-pleasing behavior, or the more intense fawning mode, is a kind of social trauma response.

This tendency to please others means you often overlook your need for self-care until you reach a state of crisis. Recognizing burnout or crisis can be difficult when you have a disconnection from your sense of self (see the previous topic). And then prioritizing self-care and setting boundaries may be challenging as they go against your people-pleasing nature! These issues stack on top of one another in complex ways, and it often takes something catastrophic before you're willing to take your needs seriously!

Can you think of a time when you engaged in people-pleasing behaviors instead of meeting your own needs? What did it cost you? You can write your thoughts here.

In addition to unmasking, many of us benefit from addressing these deep-seated patterns by working on boundaries and self-advocacy. For more tips on this, see Chapter 8.

STRAIN ON THE PREFRONTAL CORTEX

Autistic people often move through the social world with the help of the prefrontal cortex. This part of the brain, which is responsible for complex thinking and high-level cognitive tasks like analytical thinking and decision-making, acts as your brain's command center. Managing all these tasks requires a lot of energy, so the more you use your prefrontal cortex, the more energy you expend.

Allistic brains process social cues and context instinctively (subcortically), whereas Autistic people must use the prefrontal cortex to actively decode body language, words, and tones while simultaneously monitoring our own responses. This makes social interactions much more exhausting because they require significant cognitive effort.

 Think of it this way: For us, socializing is like running a high-demand software program during every interaction. Allistic people's social software operates quietly and efficiently in the background, allowing them to socialize on "low-power mode." In contrast, our social software requires constant, active, and hypervigilant management, which drains our batteries much faster.

The significant energy expenditure required for social processing explains why socializing can be particularly draining for many of us. The demands placed on the prefrontal cortex contribute to the overall exhaustion experienced during social encounters.

Do these thoughts about social interactions resonate with you in any way? Write some of your experiences here.

THE "MASKING PARADOX"

Masking creates a paradox where you might seem like you're coping well on the outside, but underneath, significant challenges often go unnoticed. This can lead to underdiagnosis or misdiagnosis because your real struggles aren't recognized.

If Autistic people appear "too normal" due to masking, people may doubt that they need accommodations, leading to needs being dismissed or invalidated. Masking consumes a lot of energy, and paradoxically, the more you mask, the harder it becomes to get the support you need. This creates a dangerous cycle: The more you mask, the more internal stress you accumulate, but you appear to need less help, which leads to even less support, until you hit a crisis point. Masking makes it harder to access diagnosis and necessary supports and accommodations, intensifying burnout and worsening mental health challenges.

This is one of the most significant costs of masking—how it makes it harder to get the accommodations you need for handling daily stressors. This limits your capacity to manage life's challenges. When you lack proper accommodations at work, at school, or for your sensory needs, your ability to cope with stress weakens (your bucket is smaller). Yet, for those who mask, getting these accommodations is often a struggle, as your needs are often misunderstood, underestimated, and invalidated.

Now that you've learned about this paradox, do you see it operating in any areas of your life? Where, and how?

OVERRIDING YOUR NATURAL INSTINCTS TO SELF-SOOTHE

Masking teaches us to override and suppress our natural instincts for self-soothing, causing us to lose access to self-soothing and, more problematically, to distrust our bodies' signals. When we mask, we suppress many of the things our bodies want to do to soothe us, such as swaying, rocking, flapping, or avoiding eye contact. By continually suppressing behaviors, we learn to ignore what our bodies are telling us we need. We learn that meeting social expectations is more important than our bodies' signals.

For example, you might accept hugs even if they feel intrusive, or you might stop moving your body because you fear it looks odd. This constant self-policing sends a harmful message: **"I can't trust my body's signals about what feels good or safe."** Your cues for safety get thwarted, which not only exacerbates burnout but also places you in vulnerable positions. The ability to trust your body's signals is foundational to identifying unsafe situations and people and moving toward safety.

Overriding these signals also adds stress to your system while simultaneously restricting access to the self-soothing behaviors that would help release this stress. This suppression contributes to an increased overall stress burden.

Can you think of a time when you suppressed a self-soothing practice in order to make others feel more comfortable? What behaviors did you override and why? Write about the situation here.

Two Tactics for More Mindful Masking

Though masking can lead to chronic burnout, unmasking is not stress-free either. Many of us experience the stress of absorbing others' emotional discomfort and responding to stigma and stereotypes when we unmask. It is tempting to fall into the simplistic narrative: "Just unmask" and all will be well. But it's not quite that simple. Trying to do the following two things can support mindful unmasking:

❶ Develop the Ability to Unmask While Alone

Masking often develops early in life and becomes an unconscious part of your psyche. Unmasking, on the other hand, is about learning who you are. While it may not be safe for everyone to unmask publicly, my hope is that all Autistic people can unmask in the comfort of privacy. In that private space, you have more freedom to explore your desires and needs and to move your body in ways that soothe and comfort you.

Do you have a space where you feel safe to unmask? Where is it? Describe the location and how you feel while you're there.

_____

_____

_____

❷ Be More Strategic and Thoughtful in Your Use of Masking

There will be times in your life when being unmasked would cause more stress than masking. Until we create a world where all neurotypes are accepted, the goal is to become more intentional and value driven in choosing when to mask. The point is to increase agency. Masking can be conceptualized as a social trauma response, and often happens unconsciously without conscious awareness. Using masking as a tool you can choose to deploy or not is one way of reclaiming agency and empowerment. For example, next time you feel the urge to quiet your jittery foot or force eye contact, ask yourself, "Do I really need to override my body's instincts right now?"

Can you think of a space where you currently automatically mask—but maybe you do not need to do that in the future?

_____

_____

_____

Gentle Unmasking

Unmasking, or as I prefer to call it, "unearthing" (a term introduced by Seren Sterling, an Autistic life coach with ADHD), is deeply personal and looks different for everyone. Kieran Rose, an Autistic author, public speaker, and researcher, cautions that within the Autistic community, the pressure to present in a certain way can create a new kind of mask. For example, the pressure to appear stereotypically Autistic might lead someone to adopt new "Autistic" characteristics, which is just another form of conforming.

The process of unearthing is about coming to know yourself. Masking makes it hard to know your true self, your delights, and your pleasures. **Anything that brings you closer to yourself is an act toward unmasking.** I encourage people to start unmasking by anchoring into two principles: **pleasure** and **play**.

THE PLAY PRINCIPLE

Play allows you to rediscover and embrace parts of yourself that may have been abandoned in early childhood.

THE PLEASURE PRINCIPLE

Discovering what brings you pleasure and delight, then learning to take those things seriously, is a powerful way to learn about yourself.

WHAT IS THE PLAY PRINCIPLE?

Why Play?

Play is the crucible in which we become ourselves . . . . It's the space of identity exploration and formation.

Play is where we experiment, explore,
and discover what brings us joy.

The renowned theorist, pediatrician, and psychoanalyst Dr. Donald W. Winnicott believed that play was where we discover the self. Play helps kids learn differentiation (what is me and what is not me).

But wait . . . take a minute to think about how play gets stunted for many Autistic children.

Stunted Play Leads to Stunted Identity Formation

The way Autistic children enjoy play is often not considered "normative" or healthy. This means, **as a child, your play may have been disrupted** or discouraged, or you may have learned to mask your natural forms of play. And this is no small thing—play is serious developmental business. **Through play, children form and develop a sense of self** and learn about themselves and the world. Unfortunately, this process is often thwarted for many Autistic people.

Many of us develop what I call "play shame"—feeling ashamed of how we play. Since play and self are so interconnected, this shame affects your ability to flourish and find your true self.

Reflecting on Your Experience with Play

Winnicott believed that play helps children explore their identities and is the place we discover who we are. Think about that concept as you write down your responses to these prompts.

What words or emotions come to mind when you think of play?

_____

_____

_____

_____

Can you remember your first memory of playing?

_____

_____

_____

Did you ever experience shame associated with play?

_____

_____

_____

In your memories (past and recent) were you playing alone or with others?

_____

_____

_____

What themes do you notice in your play?

_____

_____

_____

_____

_____

How easy or difficult is it for you to access play now?

_____

_____

_____

_____

What was your most recent experience of play, and how was that for you? What memories or associations come to mind when you think of play?

_____

_____

_____

_____

How Do You Like to Play?

By getting back in touch with play and the playful part of yourself, you can resume aspects of your identity exploration and formation that may have gotten thwarted or abandoned in early childhood. However, play often comes less naturally once you're no longer a young child. Here are some examples of ways to play to spark your imagination. Check any that interest you, and add your own ideas in the blank spots.

CREATIVE ARTS

- Drawing, painting, sculpting
- Crafting or DIY projects
- Writing stories or poetry
- Playing a musical instrument

OTHER:
- _____

SOCIAL PLAY

- Role-playing games (e.g., Dungeons & Dragons)
- Improv or acting classes
- Participating in cosplay events

OTHER:
- _____
- _____

INTERESTS AND PASSIONS

- Diving into your interests and passions
- Pursuing lifelong learning through courses or workshops
- Volunteering for causes aligned with your passions or values

OTHER:
- _____
- _____
- _____

GAMES AND PUZZLES

- Board games or card games
- Video games
- Jigsaw puzzles or logic puzzles
- Escape rooms

OTHER:
- _____

NOSTALGIC ACTIVITIES

- Revisiting childhood hobbies or interests
- Re-engaging with favorite shows, movies, or books from childhood
- Building with LEGO® or other construction toys

OTHER:
- _____
- _____

NATURE PLAY

- Exploring forests, mountains, or beaches as your playground
- Hiking or nature walks
- Nature photography

OTHER:
- _____

PHYSICAL PLAY

- Dancing
- Martial arts, yoga, or Pilates
- Rhythmic movement like rollerblading, swimming, jumping rope, or swinging
- Playing sports or engaging in repetitive movement

OTHER:
- _____

SENSORY PLAY

- Engaging in tactile activities like clay modeling or sand play
- Listening to music or creating soundscapes
- Exploring different textures and materials

OTHER:
- _____

SLOW PLAY

- Gardening or tending to plants
- Playing with pets or animals
- Adult coloring books or mandala art

OTHER:
- _____

Make a Play Plan

In our busy modern lives, it can be difficult to find time to play. Here are a few tips for fitting play into your life. Check any that might work for you, and add your own ideas in the blank spaces.

○ *Schedule playtime every day or week like you would any other appointment. This will help you prioritize play as you do with other important tasks.*

○ *Incorporate play into an activity you already do or that's already happening around you. For example, join your children as they finger-paint, or use dance as a form of exercise.*

○ *Try parallel play! Parallel play is when we engage in play alongside others doing a similar task (for example both painting, or both building with LEGO®).*

○

○

○

○

○

○

WHAT IS THE PLEASURE PRINCIPLE?

Why Pleasure?

Many people who mask develop hypersensitive "antennae" to detect what other people want and desire, including what other people want them to be.

When your radio signal is sensitively cued into the signals of others, **it becomes difficult to cue into your own signals** and know what you truly find pleasure in. Thinking "I want whatever will make you happy with me!" leads to a diffuse sense of self (a lack of self-identity).

Additionally, many of us have learned to feel embarrassed about our special interests and pleasures, leading to a further disconnect from what brings us joy.

The pleasure principle is the process of getting in touch with your pleasure and delight and learning to take your pleasure seriously. To help the learning process, ask yourself questions like these. If you want, jot down your responses in the spaces provided.

What kind of movement gives me pleasure?

_____

_____

_____

What sort of social connection delights me?

_____

_____

_____

What does my ideal evening look like?

_____

_____

_____

How much social contact is enjoyable?

_____

_____

_____

What sensory experiences bring me delight?

_____

_____

_____

Reflecting on What Brings You Pleasure

Many of us have learned to suppress our desires or avoid the things that soothe us. Think about that concept as you write down your responses to these prompts.

Do you suppress your desires or avoid what soothes you to meet the expectations of others? How so?

_____

_____

_____

Can you recall a recent moment of pleasure? What was it?

_____

_____

_____

Do you find that certain senses (like touch, taste, or smell) more readily bring you pleasure? Which ones, and in what ways?

_____

_____

_____

How comfortable are you with sharing your desires and pleasures with others?

_____

_____

_____

What experiences are pleasurable for you? What soothes you?

_____

_____

_____

When you think about your relationship to pleasure, what memories, details, or associations come to mind (e.g., do you feel excited, guilty, etc.)?

_____

_____

_____

What movement(s) feels good? Consider experimenting with new movements (swaying, pacing, dancing, jumping) to learn what movements feel pleasurable.

_____

_____

_____

Play + Pleasure = Gentle Unmasking

Unmasking can feel like an overwhelming and complex task, making it hard to start. So, if you're feeling lost, keep this simple equation in mind:

Play + Pleasure = GENTLE UNMASKING

By leaning in with curiosity to explore what genuinely delights you, you can begin to unearth your authentic self. In essence, you're striving to reconnect with yourself beneath the layers of conditioning and performance. It's a journey back to your true self, guided by the things that bring you genuine joy, connection, and delight.

This chapter will conclude with worksheets to help you think through how to care for yourself when you do mask. There will likely be situations where you decide to mask if you are able, such as social events or job interviews, because it feels less stressful than dealing with the fallout of unmasking. These worksheets are designed to help you navigate those decisions with more care.

Follow your curiosity all the way home to yourself.

The first worksheet introduces you to a "double pros and cons table," a tool commonly used in dialectical behavior therapy (DBT), a therapy type developed by Dr. Marsha Linehan. A double pros and cons table helps you think about a situation from both perspectives (if you do something and if you don't) and list the pros and cons of each option. This creates a four-section visual that allows you to weigh the pros and cons of each scenario. My friend and colleague Samantha Ascanio, who runs a DBT clinic, inspired the idea of employing this commonly used DBT technique for Autistic masking. With her permission, I've adapted it for exploring the pros and cons of masking.

You'll find an example of how this exercise can be applied to Autistic masking, followed by a template for you to use. Additionally, there is a worksheet that offers a framework for creating a self-care plan for high-masking situations or days.

Masking Double Pros and Cons Table

This a tool for evaluating decisions by considering both the benefits and drawbacks of masking and of not masking.

EXAMPLE SCENARIO: *Attending a friend's baby shower*

MASKING

PROS

Privacy and control: I can manage how I am perceived by people I don't know.

Blending in: I won't stand out as different and attract unwanted attention.

Less anxiety: There will be less immediate anxiety about how I come across.

Emotional tone: I won't have to absorb the emotional discomfort of others.

CONS

Energy: I'll likely be more tired and exhausted afterward.

Inauthentic connections: It will be harder to bond authentically with others.

Touch: More people may touch me or ask for hugs.

Internal strain: I will experience increased internal stress from suppressing self-soothing.

NOT MASKING

PROS

Energy: The event will be less exhausting.

Authenticity: I know when someone connects with me, it will be genuine.

Advocacy: Being visibly Autistic is a form of advocacy I embrace.

Needs seen: It will be easier to ask for what I need, like taking sensory breaks.

CONS

Rumination: I might ruminate about how I came across to others.

Emotional tone: I will pick up on others' discomfort, which is overwhelming.

Risk of conflict: There's a possibility of conflict if people misunderstand my behavior.

Worries about perception: I'm concerned about being seen as different or not being invited again.

VALUES

When considering whether to mask or not, reflect on the values that come up, such as:

- Belonging
- Authenticity
- Connection

Note that these values may exist in conflict.

INTERNAL BARRIERS

When considering whether to mask or not, reflect on the internal barriers that bubble up:

- Worries about being seen as different
- Worries that my friend will never invite me to another event

Barriers identified are often access points for deeper exploration of internalized ableism, grief of limits, and other emotional challenges related to navigating one's neurodivergence.

PLAN

Modified approach: Attend the event for a shorter amount of time, mostly mask, but take sensory breaks and explain if asked. This balances masking to reduce anxiety while allowing for some authenticity and self-care.

Masking Double Pros and Cons Table

The situation I'm considering is ....
....

List the pros and cons of masking, and then create a
separate list of pros and cons for not masking.

MASKING

PROS

CONS

NOT MASKING

PROS

CONS

VALUES

*When considering whether to mask or not,
reflect on the values that come up, such as:*

INTERNAL BARRIERS

*When considering whether to mask or not,
reflect on the internal barriers that bubble up:*

PLAN

Tips for Managing High-Masking Days

For situations that require a lot of masking, create a self-care plan for before, during, and after the event. This approach helps you enter the situation feeling prepared and grounded, ensures you have support during the event, and provides downtime to decompress afterward. Following are some ideas that can help you during each phase. Check off the ones that might work for you.

BEFORE

- ◯ *Allow time to set yourself up well.*
- ◯ *Engage in some sensory soothing activities.*
- ◯ *Plan ahead and gather supplies.*
- ◯ *Create any scripts that may help you (especially exit scripts or boundary scripts).*

DURING

- ◯ *Bring and use sensory supports.*
- ◯ *Take breaks.*
- ◯ *Have scripts available.*
- ◯ *Know your exit plan.*

AFTER/RECOVERY

- ◯ *Engage in a sensory detox ritual.*
- ◯ *Complete the stress cycle.*
- ◯ *Draw upon comfort items (objects that soothe your system).*
- ◯ *Use safe foods.*
- ◯ *Draw on weighted items that help with grounding.*
- ◯ *Maintain high control during this period.*

Make a Self-Care Plan for High-Masking Days

Fill in ideas that will work for you.

BEFORE

- ○ _____
- ○ _____
- ○ _____
- ○ _____
- ○ _____
- ○ _____

DURING

- ○ _____
- ○ _____
- ○ _____
- ○ _____
- ○ _____
- ○ _____

AFTER/RECOVERY

- ○ _____
- ○ _____
- ○ _____
- ○ _____
- ○ _____
- ○ _____

CHAPTER 8

Establishing Accommodations and Boundaries

Using Self-Advocacy to Minimize Burnout

A core part of building a life resilient to burnout involves learning to say no, setting limits, and ensuring appropriate accommodations are in place. The lack of these skills and supports is a significant factor driving many of us to burnout.

As you may recall from Chapter 1, **burnout happens when demands exceed your capacity**. When you have accommodations in place, you increase your capacity (you give yourself a larger bucket). Practicing good boundaries helps you manage the flow (reduce the amount coming out of the faucet). **The ability to confidently self-advocate is the foundation that enables you to build accommodation plans** and set boundaries effectively.

This chapter dives into the importance of self-advocacy, how to get accommodations, and tips for boundary setting. I'll give you the how, but keep in mind there is often deeper psychological work to be done as part of this process. For example, we often have to address:

Impostor syndrome around our identity and diagnosis

Deep-seated people-pleasing, fawn-response, and masking behaviors

Internalized ableism (which creates discomfort with accepting accommodations)

While this chapter provides the practical steps, I hope you'll also **consider finding a therapist, friend, or neurodivergent community to help you work through the deeper issues** that often need to be addressed alongside learning the how-to of self-advocacy.

WHAT IS

Autistic Self-Advocacy?

"Self-advocacy" can sound like a big and intimidating word. The first time I heard it, I pictured myself at a protest (and protests don't jive with my sensory system!). But self-advocacy doesn't have to be big and loud—it can be as simple as **making a request of another person** or asking for the lighting to be adjusted.

Autistic people often struggle with self-advocacy, and this makes sense for several reasons:

> ▶ Rejection sensitivity

> ▶ Shame around our distinct needs

> ▶ Fawn/trauma responses

> ▶ Desire to blend in and not stand out

> ▶ Uncertainty about how to word requests

> ▶ Previous efforts at self-advocacy being dismissed as "rude"

Many of us expend a tremendous amount of energy just trying to blend in. Self-advocacy requires us to center *our* needs, which by nature demands we stand out a bit. Additionally, whether due to interoception challenges or masking, many of us have difficulty **identifying what we need**. Our ability to self-advocate may have been discouraged or trained out of us, as early attempts—such as saying "get away from me"—may have been perceived as rude by others.

Another factor that makes self-advocacy challenging is that we may not know how to do it—what to say, what to ask for, or how to express our needs effectively. The pragmatics, or the "how," of self-advocacy can be difficult for many of us. On the next page, we'll dive into practices for identifying your needs. After that, we'll break down the "self-advocacy equation"—a simple way to approach expressing and communicating those needs.

Increasing Awareness of Your Needs

Self-advocacy starts with self-attunement, or the ability to attune to your needs. If we don't know what we need, we can't advocate for what we need! Here are a few ways to increase awareness of your needs.

FEELINGS AND NEEDS INVENTORY

FEELING	NEED
Anxiety	Safety, reassurance, routine, clarity, calm, resolution
Frustration	Autonomy, progress, understanding
Sadness	Comfort, connection, empathy, rest
Anger	Respect, boundaries, fairness, control, alignment (with values or principles)
Loneliness	Social connection, belonging, support
Overwhelm	Space, sensory regulation, rest, help, simplification
Fear	Security, reassurance, predictability
Guilt	Forgiveness, self-compassion, repair, values-realignment
Boredom	Engagement, stimulation, variety

Emotions are powerful signals—they are excellent communicators if you allow yourself to listen. When you notice an emotion, consider it an invitation to ask: "What do I need right now?" Over time, this practice will help you strengthen your ability to identify your needs.

"WHAT WOULD HELP RIGHT NOW?" REFLECTION

Here is an additional exercise to increase your awareness of your needs. When you feel overwhelmed or stressed, take a moment to ask yourself: "What would help me feel better right now?" Don't worry if the answer isn't perfect—just practice brainstorming options like rest, space, food, or talking to someone. If you're unsure, run through a quick checklist of basic needs using the **HALT-BS method: Hungry, Angry, Lonely, Tired (or Thirsty), Bored, Stressed (or Sensory Stressed)**. This simple self-check-in can help you identify what might be affecting you in the moment. To make it a habit, set reminders or pair this practice with an activity you already do daily. Over time, you'll build the "muscle" of self-awareness and get better at identifying and addressing your needs in real time.

The Self-Advocacy Equation

Because self-advocacy can be so daunting, I like simplifying this concept into a straightforward equation, which makes it easy to remember:

$$\text{Self-Disclosure} + \text{Request} = \textbf{SELF-ADVOCACY}$$

DO I HAVE TO SELF-DISCLOSE?

Self-disclosure isn't technically always necessary. You could simply make a request without explanation, like "Can we take this conversation outside?" or "Can you turn down the music?"

However, requests tend to be better received when paired with a stated need. In other words, you are more likely to get a favorable response from people when your requests are accompanied by an explanation of your need. That's why I've put these together in the self-advocacy equation.

DIFFERENT LEVELS OF SELF-DISCLOSURE

The self-disclosure part of the equation means that self-advocacy often involves sharing personal information about yourself. This disclosure can vary in depth; it could be a full self-disclosure ("I am Autistic") or a partial self-disclosure ("I have sensory sensitivities").

Since there are different levels of self-disclosure statements, you can choose what to share based on what's needed in various situations. The key is to share an amount of information that:

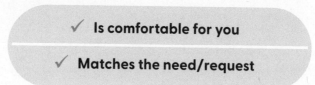

✓ Is comfortable for you

✓ Matches the need/request

The Self-Disclosure Thermometer

Self-disclosure doesn't have to be all or nothing. It's easy to think you have to either tell people you're Autistic or not say anything at all, but that's not the case. There's plenty of room for partial self-disclosures.

For instance, a partial self-disclosure could be: "I have auditory sensitivities." This allows you to share relevant information without revealing everything. It also lets you test the waters—how a person responds to a partial self-disclosure can give you insight into how they might react to a full self-disclosure.

To help you think about different levels of disclosure, I've created the self-disclosure thermometer. This tool visually guides you through various levels of vulnerability, so you can decide what you're comfortable sharing about yourself.

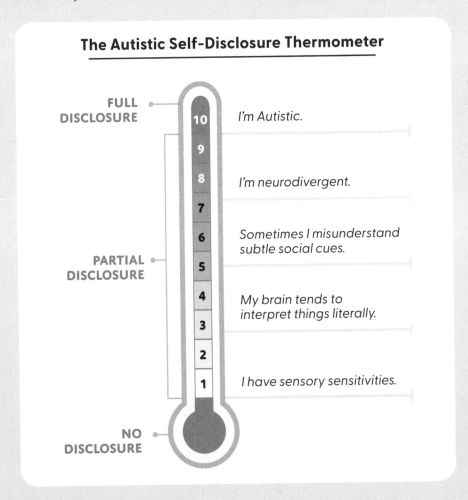

The Autistic Self-Disclosure Thermometer

FULL DISCLOSURE — 10 — I'm Autistic.

9
8 — I'm neurodivergent.
7
6 — Sometimes I misunderstand subtle social cues.

PARTIAL DISCLOSURE — 5
4 — My brain tends to interpret things literally.
3
2
1 — I have sensory sensitivities.

NO DISCLOSURE

Fill In Your Own Self-Disclosure Thermometer

Create your own hierarchy of self-disclosure.

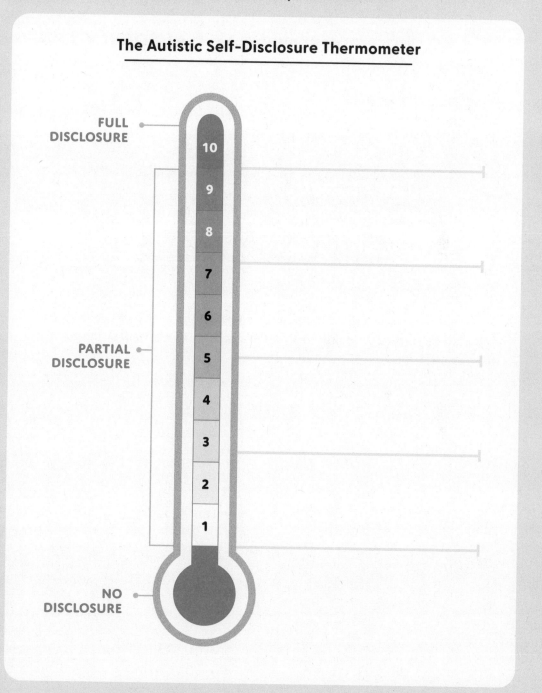

The Autistic Self-Disclosure Thermometer

FULL
DISCLOSURE

10
9
8
7
6

PARTIAL
DISCLOSURE

5
4
3
2
1

NO
DISCLOSURE

More on Self-Advocacy

Self-Disclosure **+** Request **=** SELF-ADVOCACY

WHY DISCLOSE AT ALL?

Self-disclosure (full or partial) can exist on its own for various reasons. For example, you might choose to self-disclose in order to:

Build connections by sharing more of yourself with others

Communicate proactively about a part of your identity

Give people context for your actions

Educate others and expand people's awareness of autism

When paired with a request, self-disclosure is a form of self-advocacy. A good self-advocacy statement pairs a relevant need with a level of self-disclosure that feels comfortable.

Phrasing Your Request

Self-Disclosure ✚ Request **=** **SELF-ADVOCACY**

Now, let's turn to the second part of the equation: the request. Following are two examples of how to pair self-disclosure and requests as a form of self-advocacy.

EXAMPLE A

CONTEXT: *having an in-depth conversation with a person and there is a lot of background noise*

SELF-DISCLOSURE

"**I have auditory processing difficulties,** and it is a bit difficult for me to hear in here. **Is it okay if we go sit in the booth over there,** away from the noise?"

REQUEST

....

EXAMPLE B

CONTEXT: *asking for an informal accommodation at work*

SELF-DISCLOSURE

"**I have light sensitivities and get migraines** from overhead fluorescent lighting. **Can I wear a hat at work** as this helps reduce the light exposure?"

REQUEST

The Self-Advocacy Script Library

Here are some sample requests you could use as is, or edit to fit your needs.

Phone Calls

- *I communicate more effectively through email. Can we follow up with a written summary?*

- *I do best with clear instructions. Could you repeat that to ensure I've got it right?*

- *I do best with structured discussions. Could we outline the key points before diving in?*

Social Events

- *I need a break from the noise. Can we find a spot away from the loud music to continue this conversation?*

- *I have sensory sensitivities and will need sensory breaks. Could we plan for some downtime during the event?*

- *I do best with structured activities. Can we incorporate games that have clear rules?*

Work Meetings

- *I often need to move my body and look away to focus. Would it be okay if I stood and moved during our meetings?*

- *I take in information best when it's summarized. Could we go over the main points at the end for clarification?*

- *I have some memory struggles and find it helpful to review summarized information. Would it be all right if I recorded this meeting so that my AI tool can create summary notes?*

Educational Settings

- *I learn better with visual aids. Can we incorporate more diagrams or illustrations during the lesson?*

- *I absorb information better through practical examples. Could we integrate more real-life applications into the lesson?*

- *I find it helpful to summarize key points. Can we recap the main concepts after discussing each section?*

Job Interviews

- *I tend to think better with a quiet environment. Is it possible to have the interview in a less noisy area?*

- *I thrive with a bit of flexibility. Can we allow room for follow-up questions or discussion on certain topics?*

- *I do best when I know what to expect. Can you give me a brief rundown of what the job interview will entail?*

- *I am a thoughtful processor and do well when I know what to expect. Is it possible to get a copy of the interview questions before the interview?*

Write Your Own Self-Advocacy Script

This page provides a template for you to write out your own request. You can practice this with a situation from the past, or use it for something that's upcoming.

Consider a situation where you would benefit from an adjustment (a different table, a change of lighting, asking someone to be more explicit in their communication).

SITUATION

Figure out your unmet need in the situation (is it a sensory need, a communication need, or something else?).

UNMET NEED

Decide how much you're comfortable sharing (partial disclosure, full disclosure). Write out your self-disclosure. (Be mindful to match the self-disclosure to your need. For example, if it's about communication, explain your communication style. If it's sensory related, share about your sensory experiences.)

SELF-DISCLOSURE STATEMENT

Consider what request could support you. In the space here, write out your request.

MY REQUEST

Accommodations?

Basically, **an accommodation is anything that helps your environment better adapt to your needs**. Accommodations don't have to be big and fancy, and they can be both formal and informal.

Legal Protections

While it differs by country, **most nations legally protect certain rights and reasonable accommodations for disabled people**. In the US, autism is protected under the Americans with Disabilities Act. Using this designation often requires an official medical diagnosis, and you might have to submit paperwork to your institution or workplace. However, this information is confidential and protected by law.

Deciding Not to Pursue Legally Protected Accommodations

While these rights are protected, **many people choose not to disclose at work due to ongoing stigma** and fear of potential backlash. In fact, a 2022 survey found that only 30 percent of Autistic employees had disclosed their autism to their human resources department. Additionally, many other Autistic individuals are either awaiting diagnosis or choosing not to pursue a formal diagnosis.

When weighing the pros and cons of a formal diagnosis, the role of legal protections often plays a key part. Some people may be able to get the accommodations they need through a different diagnosis (for example, if they have a pre-existing diagnosis of ADHD or a medical condition that offers similar accommodations). In such cases, they may choose to pursue accommodations under that diagnosis rather than pursuing a formal autism accommodation or disclosure.

Examples of Formal Accommodations

Formal accommodations are adjustments that you request from your employer, school, or other institutions, and they are protected under legal rights. They typically require a medical diagnosis of autism. Here are a few examples of formal accommodations you may qualify for:

FLEXIBLE WORK OR SCHOOL HOURS: *Adjusting start and end times to accommodate personal productivity patterns*

QUIET AND REMOTE WORKSPACES: *Access to low-stimulation areas to enhance focus and reduce sensory overload and/or the option to work remotely when job tasks allow*

SENSORY-FRIENDLY ENVIRONMENT: *Permission to use sensory supports such as noise-canceling headphones or dimmed lighting or to take sensory breaks*

COMMUNICATION ACCOMMODATIONS: *Option to communicate via email or text instead of in-person meetings or phone calls*

ASSISTIVE TECHNOLOGY: *Access to assistive technology such as readers, note-taking software, and speech-to-text software*

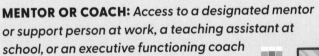

MENTOR OR COACH: *Access to a designated mentor or support person at work, a teaching assistant at school, or an executive functioning coach*

Examples of Informal Accommodations

Informal accommodations are accommodations that you build into your life that aren't connected to your workplace or school and have nothing to do with legal protections—but they are still very valuable! For instance, I often wear a beanie (hat), even though it's not typical professional attire. The proprioceptive input from the beanie helps me feel grounded and more regulated. This is an example of an informal accommodation I give myself.

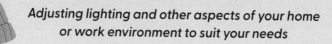

Saying no to plans (Tip: It might be easier to say no if you think of this as an accommodation you're giving yourself)

Getting a food-delivery service or other supports to help with food prep

Using sensory support tools

Adjusting lighting and other aspects of your home or work environment to suit your needs

Resources for More Learning

There are some excellent resources for learning more about accommodations and self-advocacy. Here are a few that provide valuable information, tools, directories, and more.

- ▶ **Autistic Self Advocacy Network (ASAN):** *https://autisticadvocacy.org*

- ▶ **Autistic Women & Nonbinary Network (AWN):** *https://awnnetwork.org*

- ▶ **Neurodiversity Network:** *https://neurodiversitynetwork.net*

- ▶ **Job Accommodation Network (JAN):** *https://askjan.org*

Accommodations and Internalized Ableism

One of the main obstacles to obtaining accommodations is our internalized ableism. Internalized ableism occurs when you adopt negative views about disability, leading to shame. Additionally, the fear of standing out presents an obstacle, as you may wish to avoid standing out to prevent stress and discrimination. You may also feel that the potential safety risks associated with standing out make the accommodations seem not worth requesting. For this reason, it can be helpful to weigh the pros and cons of using an accommodation.

Chapter 7 outlines the concept of a double pros and cons table and its usefulness in deciding whether or not to mask. We're going to use one here to explore accommodations. A double pros and cons table helps you evaluate a situation from both perspectives (if you do something and if you don't) by listing the pros and cons of each option. This creates a four-section visual that allows you to weigh the benefits and drawbacks of each scenario. My friend and colleague Samantha Ascanio, who frequently adapts dialectical behavior therapy tools for Autistic clients, inspired this idea. With her permission, I've built on her idea to create the following worksheets to explore the pros and cons of using an accommodation.

Accommodation Double Pros and Cons Table

This a tool for evaluating decisions by considering both the benefits and drawbacks of seeking an accommodation and not seeking an accommodation.

EXAMPLE SCENARIO: *Deciding whether to request an accommodation for university housing*

ACCOMMODATION	Requesting a solo-dorm accommodation from my university

PROS

Privacy and control: *I'll have my own space to manage as I like.*

Sensory regulation: *I can adjust my surroundings for sensory needs.*

Uninterrupted focus: *I'll be able to study or relax without distractions.*

Better sleep: *I'll have a quiet environment for better sleep.*

CONS

Unwanted questions: *I may need to explain my situation to people who ask.*

Social connection: *It will be harder to bond with my dorm mates.*

Feeling of isolation: *Living alone might lead to feelings of loneliness or isolation.*

NO ACCOMMODATION	Using the standard dormitory-matching process to find a roommate

PROS

Blend in: *I won't stand out as different.*

Traditional experience: *Having a roommate offers a traditional college experience.*

Social opportunities: *It may be easier to meet people and make friends.*

Support system: *Having someone for mutual support and companionship could be valuable.*

CONS

Noise and mess: *There is the potential for loud or messy living conditions.*

Sensory overload: *Increased sensory input from shared spaces could be overwhelming.*

Limited privacy: *I will have less personal space.*

Risk of conflict: *There is the possibility of not getting along with my roommate.*

VALUES

Consider values embedded in this decision, with particular attention to value clashes:

- Belonging
- Self-care

Note that these values may exist in conflict.

INTERNAL BARRIERS

Reflect on any hesitations or doubts that might be affecting your decision:

- Worry about being seen as different
- Worry that I might miss out on the college experience
- Uncertainty whether I truly "need" this

Barriers identified are often access points for deeper exploration of internalized ableism, grief of limits, or other complex emotions related to your neurodivergence.

PLAN

I will request a solo dorm accommodation to prioritize my privacy and sensory needs, and I'll make sure to stay socially engaged by joining a club or group that aligns with my interests or identity.

Accommodation Double Pros and Cons Table

The situation I'm considering is ....
....

List the pros and cons of seeking the accommodation, and then create a separate list of pros and cons for not seeking the accommodation.

ACCOMMODATION

PROS	CONS

NO ACCOMMODATION

PROS	CONS

VALUES	INTERNAL BARRIERS
Consider values embedded in this decision, with particular attention to value clashes:	*Reflect on any hesitations or doubts that might be affecting your decision:*

PLAN

Setting and Maintaining Boundaries

Boundaries are the essential markers that define who you are, outlining where your identity, values, and sense of self begin and end. They help you make decisions that reflect what's important to you, guiding where to invest your time and energy. Healthy boundaries provide a secure container that allows you to engage with the world in a way that honors your intentions and respects your limits. Healthy boundaries communicate safety and containment and are not used to punish. Understanding and creating boundaries is particularly important during Autistic burnout recovery. Here are a few reasons why:

▶ **PREVENTS OVERWHELM:** Helps you manage sensory input and emotional exhaustion

▶ **PRESERVES ENERGY:** Helps you conserve energy and avoid overcommitment

▶ **BUILDS SELF-ADVOCACY SKILLS:** Encourages effective communication of personal needs

One boundary that is often misunderstood by non-Autistic people is the use of **strategic withdrawal** for managing burnout. Strategic withdrawal is a way many Autistic people manage their limited energy and sensory "spoons." While withdrawal is often seen as unhelpful avoidance or a sign of deepening depression, recent research shows that stepping back is an effective strategy that Autistic people use to manage limited energy and recover from burnout.

To practice strategic withdrawal effectively, you need to feel comfortable asserting your boundaries. Strategic withdrawal can easily be misinterpreted by those around you, which is why it's important to communicate your need for time and space clearly. It doesn't mean you're depressed or don't like the other person or people; it just means you need some personal space to recover.

Information on strategic withdrawal comes from Jane Mantzalas et al., "What Is Autistic Burnout? A Thematic Analysis of Posts on Two Online Platforms," *Autism in Adulthood* 4, no. 1 (March 2022): 52–65.

Three Steps for Setting Effective Boundaries

Sometimes the hardest part of setting boundaries is knowing your boundaries in the first place! Deciding how to communicate them can also be a challenge. This three-step process can make the task a little easier.

STEP ONE
Reflect on Your Needs

Reflect on your needs, your values, and what causes you stress or expends energy. Discovering your boundaries by understanding yourself is the foundation of setting meaningful limits.

STEP TWO
Define Your Boundaries

Clearly identify what you need to feel safe and supported. Decide on your limits in various situations, such as work, relationships, and personal time.

STEP THREE
Communicate Assertively

Share your boundaries with others in a calm and clear manner. Use "I" statements to express your needs and ensure you are understood.

Discover Your Boundaries

Creating boundaries starts with gaining clarity on what your boundaries even are! Masking often interferes with boundaries you might have created, so many of us have to discover what we need with a bit of intention. There are also many different kinds of boundaries (such as physical, personal, time, and privacy). Following are some questions to get you thinking about what your boundaries may be. Fill in any thoughts you have in the blank spaces provided.

 PHYSICAL/BODY

What are my boundaries regarding sharing my personal space with others?

_____

_____

_____

_____

_____

What actions or behaviors from others make me feel comfortable or uncomfortable in my space?

_____

_____

_____

_____

_____

What are my needs around privacy?

_____

_____

_____

_____

Are there parts of my body I don't like touched? How do I feel about hugs?

_____

_____

_____

_____

B RELATIONSHIPS

What emotional support am I willing to offer, and what are my limits?

_____

_____

_____

_____

_____

_____

How do I express my need for personal space or alone time to people close to me?

_____

_____

_____

_____

_____

_____

What behaviors or actions from others make me feel respected or disrespected in a relationship?

_____

_____

_____

_____

_____

C WORK

What tasks am I comfortable taking on, and what exceeds my capacity?

_____

_____

_____

_____

How accessible am I? Do I have specific work hours, or am I always accessible?

_____

_____

_____

What are my boundaries with checking work emails and phone calls?

_____

_____

_____

_____

What actions or behaviors from others do I find acceptable or unacceptable in the workplace?

_____

_____

_____

D PERSONAL TIME

What activities rejuvenate me, and how often do I want to engage in them?	What interruptions or disturbances do I find unacceptable during my personal time?	How much personal time do I need to feel balanced and energized?

E DIGITAL

What types of interactions or content online do I find supportive or detrimental to my well-being?	How accessible do I want to be to people through digital means (text, email, social media)?	What kind of content do I want to see, and what do I want to avoid?

Other forms of boundaries to consider thinking about include:	• Energy boundaries • Privacy boundaries • Sexual boundaries • Financial boundaries	• Emotional boundaries • Spiritual boundaries • Property/material objects boundaries

Look for Patterns

As you reflect on your responses to these prompts, what common themes or patterns do you notice about the boundaries that are important to you? For example, you might notice a pattern of prioritizing boundaries that protect your alone time or ones that help provide your life with predictability, such as boundaries around routine disruptions.

At-a-Glance Summary of Your Boundaries

Write or draw your boundaries in the spaces provided.

PHYSICAL/BODY	RELATIONSHIPS

WORK	PERSONAL TIME

DIGITAL	OTHER

Avoid Poor Boundaries

Now let's review what poor boundary language looks like. In recent years, I've observed that the term "boundaries" is often used in ways that don't actually reflect healthy boundaries, so it's useful to know what to try to avoid. Here are some examples of poor use of boundary language:

▶ **REACTIVE DISAGREEMENT:** Saying "I'm putting up a boundary" to shut down a difficult conversation. This approach avoids uncomfortable feelings rather than fostering understanding.

▶ **AVOIDING ACCOUNTABILITY:** Using "boundaries" to avoid taking responsibility. This can be a power move to dodge responsibility or difficult discussions, but boundaries shouldn't be used to avoid necessary conversations.

▶ **ANGER BOUNDARIES/WITHDRAWING AFFECTION AS PUNISHMENT:** Setting boundaries while angry and saying something like, "I need space; I'm not speaking to you for a week." That is an ultimatum or punishment, not a healthy boundary.

▶ **USING BOUNDARIES TO CONTROL:** Saying "My boundary is for you to be home at night" is controlling. Boundaries should help you meet your needs, not change or control others. Instead, you might state your intention to leave if someone continues an unhealthy behavior, focusing on your need and what you will do about it. The person then has a choice.

True boundaries are meant to communicate safety, respect, and mutual understanding. They help you protect your well-being while engaging meaningfully with others. Think of boundaries as creating a sturdy container, making relationships safe and able to endure hard conversations. Healthy boundaries communicate safety and containment, not punishment.

Tips for Setting Effective Boundaries

❶ Anchor in a Need

Anchoring the conversation in your needs can help make the conversation more successful because it encourages honest communication and helps both parties understand what truly matters. For example, "I need to rest this weekend, so I am unable to do that."

❷ Less Is More

When it comes to explaining your boundaries, saying less is often better, especially when dealing with someone who tends to resist or violate your boundaries. People who want to argue about or disrespect your boundaries will pick apart your explanations to prove they are invalid or offer solutions to change your boundaries. (Be mindful that the Autistic brain often has the urge to overexplain, making this suggestion a hard one for us.)

❸ Be Honest (and Clear)

If someone asks you to hang out or help with a project and the answer is no, don't say something like, "That won't work today, but maybe I could do it tomorrow" or "If you can't find anyone else, I guess I could." Instead, answer clearly and honestly, like, "I'm sorry, I don't have the capacity to take that on," so you don't leave any room for misinterpretation.

❹ Have Scripts On Hand

Have scripts ready for saying no. Saying no can be hard for us, and many Autistic people feel a need to overexplain and provide *all* the context. Remember, with boundaries, less is often more! Here are a few ways to say no:

- I appreciate the offer, but I can't.
- That won't work for me, but thank you for thinking of me.
- That's not something I can take on right now.

❺ Be Firm

Boundary pushers have a knack for finding people they sense will cave. These aren't the people you want to attract into your life! You can be kind and firm. When you are firm, people are less likely to push.

❻ Automate Boundaries

It's equally important to establish boundaries with yourself—and for your future self. For example, you could unfollow social media accounts that aggravate you or limit app usage at certain times to avoid doomscrolling. I think of these automated boundaries as guardrails that I create to help me act in ways that are aligned with my values and needs.

Learn from Past Experiences

Boundary making takes practice and reflection! When you encounter something that doesn't go well, **reflecting on what boundary would have been helpful and when you would have implemented it** is a great way to learn from your experience. So, practice, reflect, and practice! You can get started with the following prompts.

A recent situation where a boundary would have been helpful:

When in the process would I have wanted to set the boundary?

What was the underlying need in that situation?

What could I have said? (Or if setting a self-boundary, what guardrail could I have created?)

Reflect: How might setting the boundary have impacted the situation?

Set and Communicate Your Boundaries

Preparing for and anticipating conversations where you may need to say no or set a boundary—and coming up with a script ahead of time—can help you be more confident when these situations arise. Let's review the three-step process you learned a few pages ago to write and communicate a new boundary you want to set.

STEP ONE

Reflect on Your Needs

Reflect on your needs, your values, and what causes you stress or expends energy. Discovering your boundaries by understanding yourself is the foundation of setting meaningful limits.

_____

_____

_____

STEP TWO

Define Your Boundaries

Clearly identify what you need to feel safe and supported. Decide on your limits in various situations, such as work, relationships, and personal time.

_____

_____

_____

STEP THREE

Communicate Assertively

Share your boundaries with others in a calm and clear manner. Use "I" statements to express your needs and ensure you are understood.

_____

_____

_____

Building a Sustainable Life

Congratulations!

You've made it to the end of this workbook. I know it's a lot of information, **so please be patient with yourself** and take your time implementing these practices. Building a sustainable life, unearthing your authentic self, and addressing old patterns takes time and doesn't happen overnight.

Recovering from and preventing burnout is fundamentally about **creating a life that aligns with your nervous system, sensory system, neurodivergent energy rhythms, and needs**.

Burnout is often a symptom of a much larger problem. It signals that the life you are currently living isn't working for you. Burnout invites you to reimagine your life and build something sturdier and more expansive.

As you move forward, **focus on reclaiming your energy** and channel it into creating a life that not only works for you but also enriches you.

Index

pros and cons table, 202–4
self-care tips, 188–90, 202–6
self-soothing behaviors, 185–87, 193–94, 201–5
understanding, 181–206
Medical conditions, 19, 21, 25, 37, 59–60, 108, 137–38, 154–55, 219–20
Mental health, 14–15, 36–37, 57–61, 154, 179–82, 187–88, 192
Mindfulness
mindful check-ins, 70, 72, 79, 135, 210
mindful masking/unmasking, 189, 194–95
mindful outsourcing, 42, 45–46, 52–53
mindful practices, 42–46, 52–53, 70–72, 86, 102, 110–11, 120, 135, 152, 177–79, 189, 194–95, 218, 233

N

Needs, awareness of, 94, 96, 118–19, 131, 188–92, 209–11, 219–21
Needs, communicating, 61–63, 79, 86, 135, 209–10, 225–26, 232–35. See also Self-advocacy skills
Nervous system
autonomic nervous system, 99–100, 102
breathing exercises, 101–4, 111, 117–23, 126–27
calming activities, 121, 128
central nervous system, 99–100
energizing activities, 123
explanation of, 98–104
healthy nervous system, 104
hyperarousal and, 64, 101, 105–6, 109, 112–16
hypoarousal and, 64, 105–7, 109, 112–16
internalized ableism and, 110
managing, 54–58, 97–128
mapping, 64, 67–68, 112–16
parasympathetic nervous system, 99–104, 110, 160
peripheral nervous system, 99–100
regulating, 24, 38–40, 54–58, 64–68, 97–128
self-care and, 118–19
somatic nervous system, 99–100
state shifting, 120–21
strengthening, 58, 64, 102–4, 110–11, 125–28
stress cycle and, 124–26

sympathetic nervous system, 99–102, 104–6, 120
tracking, 110–17
vagus nerve and, 103–4, 121
visualizing, 100
window of tolerance, 64, 98, 105–17
Neurodivergent identity, 57, 65–67
Neurodivergent nervous system, 98. See also Nervous system
Neurodiversity Network, 221

P

Pacing systems, 56, 67, 130, 134–36, 147, 152
Physical exhaustion, 12–18, 22–26, 34, 107, 113, 150, 225
Physical health, 14–15, 36, 58, 67, 102, 115–16, 154–55, 179–80. See also Medical conditions
Privilege, 41, 182
Problem-solving skills, 62, 108, 140–41, 146

R

Recovery. See also Self-care
approaches to, 40–41
belonging and, 57, 67–68
boundaries and, 47, 52–53
demands and, 40–42, 45–46, 52–53
energy and, 54–68
lifestyle adjustments for, 38, 48–68
mindset work for, 65–68
outsourcing tasks, 46, 52–53
plan for, 39–68
psychological work for, 65–68
regulating nervous system, 64–68
self-advocacy tools for, 61–68
self-insight for, 63, 67–68
sensory overload and, 48–53
simple routines for, 50, 52–53
sleep routines for, 60, 67–68
strategies for, 40–68
strengths and, 62, 67–68
support for, 42–68
unmasking and, 51–53
withdrawal strategies, 42–44, 52–53
Requests, making, 209, 211, 214–18, 220–23